CW01499686

The publication of this book has been made possible thanks to the generosity of the following:

Association for Spiritualist Knowledge, Stewarton
Mr and Mrs Bob Bassett
J. Gerrard
Glasgow Association of Spiritualists
Prof Hassan Amin, LL.B, LL.M, PhD
Langside Spiritualist Church
Brenda Lawrence
London Week 1992
M. Miller
Duncan and Linda Muir
Paisley Spiritualist Church
St David's Spiritualist Church
South Wales District Council
The Temple Spiritualist Church
Christine Wandless
R. Wilson

Thanks are also given to other individuals who also contributed to the production costs.

CONTENTS

The Seeing Eye, The Feeling Heart

By

W.V. Ford, MSNU

with

L.M.Muir, FSNU

Produced on behalf of the Spiritualists' National Union by
Tudor Press (London),
27 Old Gloucester Street,
London WC1N 3XX.

First published 1993

© Will Ford

ISBN 1 874514 07 0

Printed and published by the Longdunn Press Ltd, Barton Manor, St Philips, Bristol BS2 0RL.

FOREWORD

NEW vision comes to each era when there is a particular need, and when enough effort is made to attend to that need.

In the middle of last century, Spiritualism was such a new vision. It loudly proclaimed, "There is no death!" and demonstrated through its mediumship that the personalities of those who had apparently died could still communicate with friends and relatives living in the here and now.

It never was, and it never will be enough, just to understand that there is no death. Neither is it sufficient to know that communication with the world of Spirit is possible. The declaration of Spiritualism is not simply that communication with spirit is possible, but that communion with spirit is essential.

Mediumship makes a new source of power and ability available to all men. Life becomes much more full of real meaning and purpose. A new sense of drama, a stronger feeling of romance and a higher appreciation of morality are all important aspects of the new awareness arising from man's oneness with spirit.

With this vision, the pioneers of Modern Spiritualism set out last century.

It is only with such a vision that today's Spiritualists will find themselves again. People were never intended to be the passive recipients of messages delivered in private sittings, halls and theatres. Spiritualism was never intended to be an entertainment. It is a way of life rooted in the fact of communion - spirit with spirit - which actively involves all people.

This fact of communion is not subject to change. I have lived conscious of my mediumship for more than sixty years now. I have seen Spiritualist organisations, demonstrations and attitudes change.

But the fact of communion with spirit remains.

We need again to return to the seance room, to enjoy the intimacy of Spirit, to catch again a momentary glimpse of infinity, and feel the freshening breath of purpose, motive and meaning.

We need to learn that life is the most wonderful seance of all, where Spirit speaks when we are prepared to listen.

Will Ford, MSNU

The Awakening

By Yvonne Donelon

The rays of the rising sun
Crept like fingers of flame
Over the hushed, still morning,
And with them came the promise
Of another new day, another awakening.
Birds and animals alike
Stirred in their natural habitats,
And viewed the awakening
With eyes bright, alive to
The promise of Nature.
Morning mists lifted like a
Shroud from pasture and river,
Leaving behind them the freshness
Of sparkling water — and grass,
Wet with crystal-like dew-drops.
This is the God who lives within me,
The power to bring the light
And relief of morning,
After the shadows and darkness of night.
Awake my soul with the same warmth
And vibrancy of the rising sun.
Open my eyes and heart to the
Natural and good things of life.
Let me see, and be seen with
The brightness of eye

Of believing, of knowing.
Lift the mists from my inner-self.
Let me feel the freshness of the
Dew-drop strewn grass beneath my feet.
Grant me the privilege of drinking from
The cup of everlasting life -
Of awaking to a new beginning.

Chapter One

THE STARTING POINT

HOW did my mediumship start? I suppose I was born with a special gift, the gift of sensitivity or intuition perhaps. As far as I know, no one ever told me about a life beyond death, yet I took that for granted.

How can you ever tell which events in your life are important, and which ones are not? Life unfolds endlessly through cause and effect, but who knows which trivial causes will spark off which major effects? I suppose I could say that the pattern of my life's work developed along the lines it did because my mother decided to buy a new dress for Gussie.

My sister was due to sing a solo in the choir at Mount Zion that coming Sunday. It was to be a special occasion. Of course, everything had to be just right. My mother found exactly what she was looking for in a local shop, but what she could not find when she went to pay for it was her purse. It was nowhere to be found. Together with the shopkeeper, she came to the conclusion it had been stolen.

Not being able to buy the dress paled into insignificance when she realised that the fortnight's housekeeping had been in the purse too. What started out as a pleasant hour's shopping, turned quickly into a major catastrophe.

She had to face the inevitable and break the news to my father, Vic, that the housekeeping was gone. Never a man for many words, I suppose he resigned himself to their misfortune. In true husbandly fashion, he consoled her, and promptly left for his weekly Buff's meeting with Fred Siddaway.

In likewise truly wifely fashion, Florrie and a friend, Mrs

Flowers, decided the situation required the help of a medium, a woman she knew who lived locally.

This lady oracle read the tea leaves, and obliged them with a free consultation. She told my mother her purse was burned and the money spent, but that she would gradually get her cash back from the culprit who worked at the Green Meadow. The culprit was found — and the money duly returned in instalments as predicted.

The medium had been correct. The catastrophe mellowed into a family story. From time to time, my mother and her friend attended an evening service at the Spiritualist church.

That was my family's first rather dubious contact with Spiritualism.

My seventh birthday fell on a Friday...and on the following Sunday, my sister Gussie died. She was only nine years old. I took it for granted Gussie was in heaven because I was still aware of her.

I did not become aware: I was aware. Gussie's death brought my gift of awareness to my attention and into action through everyday things. I had always been close to my elder sister, as only two years separated us. Happily for me, her death did not separate us at all.

I would be out playing with friends when I would suddenly feel an inner tug. That's the best way I can describe it — a pull. In a moment I would become aware of Gussie. At that, I would stop my game and say I had to go in now. No one else knew, but I would go up to our room and play with Gussie. I would tell her all that had been going on and sort of keep her up to date. I never felt this was unnatural in any way, or silly. It was as real and significant as anything else I did. Therein lie the roots of my mediumship.

It was nurtured, strangely enough, through a succession of absences from school brought about by illness. After a spinal illness which restricted me to a wheel chair for some time, my schooling was further interrupted by a bout of "drinking diabetes," which was finally cured by a gypsy's remedy of giving me a spoonful of melted bone marrow to drink every time I was thirsty.

However, having uncertain health at that point had two effects, I suppose. It meant my early education was imperfect, leaving me, in later years, the responsibility of teaching myself. It also gave me plenty of opportunity for quiet reflection.

Now let me tell you something of my religious background. My father was Anglican, my mother a Congregationalist. As a boy, I went with her to the Mount Zion Chapel. It was the largest, most impressive chapel in the valley, with a splendid organ and a fine choir. I loved going there. At church there were probably more men than women. That would be unusual today, but then it was full.

I used to attend Mount Zion Chapel three times each Sunday. There was also a youth meeting, and a Band of Hope for one hour on a Thursday which I wouldn't miss. In those days it was packed to capacity.

When I was eleven, the chapel held a public speaking competition. In his summing up, Mr Davis, the minister, said I had made the whole performance of speaking sound so easy that — of course! — I had to win. Well, with that experience on top of everything else, I had to think that nothing could compare with Mount Zion.

One evening when I was fourteen, I made my way to a meeting at Mount Zion Chapel. The light was suddenly clear and bright around me. I found myself standing still as I became more intensely aware of my surroundings. Everything was more vivid in the clear evening air: I could hear the organ music drifting up towards me from my chapel, the chapel I was making my way towards.

In the stillness, I was moved with a great love for that chapel. In the beauty and intensity of that moment, I knew that the chapel was somehow "mine," that I loved it, and that I would always be there.

I was wrong.

There seemed to be a change working on me. The Sunday School at chapel used to gather together at the beginning of the meeting, but later on they would break up into groups. John Picton was my teacher. A barber and confectioner in the village, he was a good teacher because he listened to what his young students thought, and drew out their talents as a result. Generally, each of us was given a verse to read out and then we were asked to talk about it, expressing our own thoughts and opinions.

On one occasion, we got round to the question, "Do we live on after death?" Each boy had his own answer, different in some way from the others. Mine was simply, "Yes, of course we do." I thought it was obvious.

After he had gone round all the boys, Mr Picton seemed ready to move on to another topic, but I stopped him. "Wait a minute, Mr Picton," I said, "you haven't told us what you think." I wanted him to get to the bottom of the matter. "I don't know," was his reply. That answer shocked me deeply: how could this man who knew so much not know that we lived on?

I found myself paying more attention to the service in chapel. We had a visiting preacher a few Sundays later, a man who constantly touched the Bible as he spoke, much to my irritation! At the end of his sermon, he lent over the Bible in the pulpit, saying: "Life after death. That's something I don't know for certain. But as Christians, I feel that we should know."

"Should know!" I thought. "How ridiculous - we do know!" And for all that I felt Mount Zion to be my chapel, I was bamboozled that important people there should be confused about such a vital issue.

I was left questioning the church I loved so much.

Yet not long after my strange, intense, experience, I was again making my way to my beloved chapel when I met a school friend. "Where are you going Will?" he shouted.

"To chapel, of course."

"Don't you want to come with me?" he said. I stopped. "Well, where are you going?" I asked.

"To the place our mothers go to," he said, "the Spiritualist church." I found myself saying all right, and away we went.

The Spiritualist church then was nothing like the chapel. The old mission hall in Yew Street had a chequered history, having been a pub and a private house in its time. It was one of three or four churches which had sprung up in the village, perhaps as a result of the losses in the Great War.

One was called the Church of Mount Pleasance, whilst another was E. T. Jones' Place — it was behind Frank the barber's shop and next to the fish shop — but they were all very modest by nature, not at all impressive like the orthodox churches. Yew Street Church was a cramped room with rows of chairs and a platform at one end. We squeezed in at the back, listening to the prayers, the reading, the talk and the medium. Our mothers were surprised, if a bit bemused, to see us at the end of their evening.

Strange to say, my friend never went back to the Spiritualist church. And stranger still, I never went back to the chapel. The change was almost complete.

Three weeks after my first, tentative visit to Yew Street, I found myself giving my first message. Like most Spiritualist churches even today, our church held an open circle. Such a circle offers people the opportunity to sit with more experienced Spiritualists and share in their developing communication with those in the world of spirit. Everyone there would sing a hymn; then someone would speak, giving a message from Spirit. Then they would sing another hymn, have another speaker, and so on.

On my first night there, I stood up, although I didn't know why. I didn't want to stand up - I just did. I wasn't in trance or anything like that. I just knew that I wanted to speak to a lady on the far side of the circle. I suddenly found myself moving towards her.

Because I had been working with my father in the mines at that time, I could recognise the picture I was seeing in my head. I was going down the mine, stripping off and picking up the tools, making my way towards the coal face. Then suddenly, all was darkness.

I saw nothing more, but heard the words "Thursday" and "No!" I heard myself saying: "Don't send Will to work on Thursday. I can see him going with two others towards the coal face. The roof is collapsing on two men and two boys."

Having delivered the message, I sat down again, feeling once more like myself. Then I forgot all about it.

It wasn't until the following Friday as I was coming home from the Castle Pit that I noticed a school friend coming from the Merthyr Vale Pit. We were both black from our work, but as he drew closer, I realised it was Will Thomas. He began to run towards me like a long-lost brother shouting: "Thank you Will! Thank you! You saved my life!" His mother insisted he stayed off work on Thursday, so he did. His butty and the other boy he worked with were killed when the roof collapsed on them.

I was awestruck. I had never met Will's mother, and didn't

know who she was or that she attended the Spiritualist meeting.

A few months later, returning from the Spiritualist church in Yew Street, I paused at the spot where, once before, I had stopped to admire the music from Mount Zion. This time it was different.

I saw no lights, heard no voices, no music, but for a moment the whole world was still. I was part of that immense stillness. I knew then without volition or thought, knew with a depth of knowing I had not experienced before, that I would dedicate my life to Spirit. For in that still moment, I had experienced communion with Spirit. That was the most significant experience of my life.

Chapter Two

COMMUNION: THE DIVINE ART OF ASSOCIATION

"ONE law, one God, one element and one far off divine event to which the whole creation moves."

Although you might not think so from the title, this chapter is all about knowing. It explains why we need to know, what we strive to know, what we are able to know and how we can perfect our knowing.

Of course, you can know on all sorts of different levels. You can know that Cardiff is the capital of Wales. You know this because you have been told it is so, and many people will agree it is true. You know that if you let go of it, a heavy object will fall to the ground. People will have told you this is the case, but you will have proved it for yourself. If you drop a pan, it inevitably falls to your feet — so watch your toes!

This second knowing differs from the first in that it is not hearsay, not based upon the word of others. It is knowledge which comes as the result of experience, and is backed by evidence or proof. Some knowledge comes to us from the use of logic and reasoning: some mathematical truths would come into this category. This kind of knowing is completely impersonal and objective. But there is another kind of knowing which seems to be at the other end of the spectrum altogether, a deeply personal and subjective sort of knowing.

There was I at the ripe old age of fourteen, perfectly certain when I looked down on my chapel that I would be there for ever. If you had asked me then, I would have said I knew that the impression I would be there for a lifetime was true. But after the second experience I was totally certain that my life was dedicated to Spirit. Sixty years later, I can confirm that the second knowing was the more correct one.

What is the difference between these two kinds of knowing? Both were intensely moving, personal experiences, yet one was right and the other wrong. The first was knowing with the heart, the emotions, if you like. It was an intuition. The second was knowing with the mind, heart and soul, as the result of what I call "Communion." That is not an easy, sweeping statement.

It is difficult to describe your soul or what you are. Suffice it to say that you have an intellect, feelings and a sense that you go beyond the restrictions of you mind and body. In that moment of communion when I felt part of all things, it was right to all things: soul, mind and feelings; that I should dedicate myself as I did. This sense of rightness and truth in the experience made my knowing certain. My life's experience has proved it to be correct.

It is this kind of knowing that is going to be explored here, but before we move on from this experience of communion, let me add one other thing.

The two experiences also differed in what was known. The first knowledge was about physical things. It was a particular church — a body of people, a building — I thought I would always attend and love. The second knowledge was of the non-physical: I would always serve Spirit. In a sense, the first knowing was not wrong, just imperfectly interpreted, for the love of God and His people and His praise has always been there: it just was not tied to one specific, physical location. The heart was correct, but the head jumped to conclusions, so to speak. In the stillness of communion, there was no jumping, just being.

Service to Spirit has no limitations. It is not restricted to particular places or people, religions or activities, as I hope we shall see as I share my thoughts and experiences with you.

Let's get down to work now that we have surveyed the different kinds of knowing. Let's look at how the whole process has evolved.

At some stage in our development, we became aware for the first time of our self. We now know, of course, that this was a very restricted degree of awareness, but how did it happen? How was self first introduced to self? The answer must be that it learned

16

about itself by responding to its environment, to all the things and experiences round about it.

All cells or germs of life are dependent upon the ability to respond to the environment. This in itself must mean there has to be a degree of sensitivity to environment or forms outside themselves, built into all cells.

Seeds which are not raised in association with environment and atmosphere or other forms of life to which they can respond remain in a state of cold, lifeless inertia; they remain seeds. And so the life force, Divine Chemist (call it what you will), continues the experiment of linking the seed with every kind of condition until the environment awakens a degree of sensitivity. If the response is not good or desirable, the experiments will continue until the desired result is achieved through the best blend.

Awareness of the self is therefore made possible because of the living entity's ability to become sensitive to life outside that self. The first conversation of self with self must follow a pattern something like this:

"That is. This is." ("That" or "this" can refer to any form of life outside the self.) The conversation continues.

"This is not me. That's not me either. And because I know I am not this and I am not that, I know that I am."

Sooner or later, through a conversation along those lines, we make our first conscious acknowledgement of our own separate existence. Through this question and answer, a line of ever-extending communication is opened up. Slowly there comes the awareness of night and day, of shape and form, cold and heat, motion and rest. Each new acknowledgement brings fresh confirmation of the conclusion of "I am," and that this "I" has a form of separate and individual existence.

The more we learn about other things, the more we learn about what we are not. That in turn helps us to know what we are. At the very simplest, we have carved out for ourselves a physical identity. As the process of questioning and answering continues, we refine that identity as something beyond the physical.

Have you ever thought what a seance really is? You probably think of it as an occasion when a group of people sit harmoniously together to communicate with Spirit. You are aware that an extra degree of sensitivity is required for this, and may even use the phrase "Reach out to Spirit." There's nothing wrong with that definition, but if I ask you to cast your mind back to your first seance, I wonder where your mind will go?

Back five years, perhaps, or ten or thirty? Yet I am asking you to go back to your very first glimmers of consciousness, to that time when the seed of your self was just beginning to stir in response to its environment. That is your first seance. That is the first occasion when in stillness and darkness you reached out with your limited powers of awareness, and touched or blended with what was around you until you understood a little more of it, and a little more of yourself. It is at your first seance that you begin to know.

Whatever your religion is to be, that is your first seance: the first of an eternal series on your path of becoming. By being still and communing with your environment, you learn. Through the same process you become increasingly aware that "I am". There comes a time, though, when this knowledge of other things and other men is not enough. Then there is little value or joy in being aware of other life unless that other life becomes aware of you too.

Pausing in our search for knowledge, we stand over-awed by the sheer profusion of life. We marvel at the over-generous abundance of nature. Bravely, we try to take in some of the immensity of nature, of life, of space and time, but we cannot keep it to ourselves. What use would that be?

And so is born the desire to communicate more fully; the desire to be; the desire for self-expression. Man wants the world to impart to him, but in return man wants to impart to the world. Man needs the world to know him, but he has a problem. He is aware of the burgeoning earth, the heavens, the boundless water, the living air, the sun, moon and stars.

Amidst this utter profusion of life, he becomes aware of a sense of his own poverty — a poverty of mind, poverty of ability for self-expression, poverty of equipment to obtain a fuller understanding and knowledge.

What can you use to help you learn more? What can you do to improve your learning capacity? How can you get knowledge across to other people? These are the questions that man the learner and man the communicator finds himself asking.

History is full of glowing examples of man's brave endeavour to explore the realms of the unknown. It will be sufficient for our purpose to use just one example, Aristotle. Here was a man possessed of one high and noble purpose — to obtain for himself and his students (and for the benefit of mankind) the greatest possible amount of knowledge. We should be doing Aristotle a grave disservice if we were to ignore the almost fatal limitations of equipment which accompanied his unprecedented attempt to open up a line of communication of scientific and philosophical knowledge.

He was compelled to fix time without a watch, to compare degrees of heat without a thermometer, to observe the heavens without a telescope, and the weather without a barometer. In short, all the facts on which the theories of modern science are based were almost wholly undiscovered when he set out on his quest for knowledge.

While it is true that the vast body of data gathered by Aristotle and his assistants became the groundwork for the progress of science — the textbook of knowledge for the next two thousand years, and one of the wonders of the work of men — it is also true that his work suffered through the lack of proper equipment. There was no telescope and so Aristotle's astronomy is a tissue of childish romance.

For the lack of a microscope, his biology wanders endlessly astray. Yet, however muddled and fuddled may have been the conclusions of early scholars, the breakthrough was achieved. Communion with life had commenced. The flow of knowledge had begun, and men were bathing in its streams.

However, even the most vitalising water can be dangerous if you get out of your depth. Knowledge enlightens; it brings its own understanding and power. That understanding can be used to provide a nourishing environment for all men's growth, but equally it can be used for the growth of a few to dominate the many. So the fruits of Aristotle's painstaking methods of research, reasoned thought, experiment and education did not yield their full promise.

The search for knowledge continued accompanied by wars, and all their plunder, strife and poverty, blood and tears. Ignorant masses looked on in helpless bewilderment and torment as leaders and masters endeavoured to use all new facts and knowledge to enhance and strengthen their own prestige and sense of power.

Yet, through the hard work of communion and then experiment, new knowledge was discovered and communicated, but the communication was restricted to the few. New knowledge was used to help the rich and powerful to become even more rich and powerful. The call of the weak became ever more feeble and helpless.

As power-drunk emperors and rulers looked down from their high places and saw that to the more astute and perceiving minds new knowledge was being revealed, they scrambled for all possible information. The knowledge thus gathered would then, in skill and cunning, be dressed or reprocessed so that afterwards it could be directed at the people in such ways and in such forms that it would meet the requirements of the ruler's personal aspirations.

It is important to ask what has gone wrong for the misuse and misrepresentation of knowledge is not only an historical fact, it is also a contemporary problem at all levels of life and in all areas of thought. "Ask and it shall be given unto you," the Bible instructs us, but perhaps it should be added that the knowledge given is no exclusive, personal possession: it is for the good of all.

We have already widened our concept of the seance far beyond a group sitting for spirit communication. We now realise that virtually every reaching out to make the unknown known is the essential process we call a seance. Now we need to do the same thing with the idea of mediumship.

An individual is not a medium if he reaches out to understand and does nothing more. A medium is one who makes contact and channels back to others what that contact is. A medium is essentially a communicator. The less he colours the contact he makes with his own thoughts, desires and aspirations, the purer and more effective his sharing with others will be.

I told you of my experience looking down on Mount Zion Chapel, and how I coloured it by adding to the outflow of my love of God, the physical notions of the church and the people. The resulting "message" was wrong. Not the second time. Then, in pure communion, the simplicity of the experience was untampered with. The message was correct.

If the lessons learned in the seance room had been applied earlier to the seance of life, how different the story of mankind would read. Knowledge must be received and communicated with absolute honesty if it is to be effective.

"Thought is the property only of those who can entertain it," said Emerson, and rightly so. Not all individuals can "entertain" all thought, but all people are entitled to gain access to what they can cope with, and no half truths should be offered to keep them exploitable or biddable. Knowledge should be used to nurture the seed of each man in order that he might grow at a pace and in a direction best suited to his innate potential.

Not all sitters in our circles are clairvoyants or philosophers; some may grow to heal or write or bring laughter, but each is encouraged in an atmosphere of love, tolerance and honesty to develop along lines particular to himself. So it should be in the seance of life.

Honesty, or the lack of it, is only one facet of the problem. As man developed a keener sense of awareness, and facts made themselves known, soon it became clear that the trouble with facts is that there are so many of them. As more and more facts become known, man more than ever feels an air of vagueness. The whole scheme of life seems more obscure and dark, more shrouded in mystery than ever before.

The whole position becomes even more ridiculous as man knows less and less about more and more. From this jungle of chaos of entangled and unexplained facts, some semblance of order and understanding has to be developed. And so the specialist takes over. To know the whole is no longer possible, and so the whole is split into many parts. The function of the specialist is to explore and gather all possible information about the part given into his charge.

Although quite a measure of success has been achieved by this system of specialised knowledge, there is a major flaw in its method. The specialist approach continually divides and separates whereas man's attempt at understanding is a consistent endeavour to unite and form a whole. This is why philosophy and religion are often at odds with science. The first two attempt to demonstrate the

21

oneness of all things, while science with its specialisms inevitably points out the differences.

Once a man knows "I am," his next question is, "What am I?" The specialist will break him down into a series of functions, a list of constituents, a repertoire of reactions, but will not come up with one all-embracing answer. That is left to the philosopher. To him the man will look for insight, reassurance, purpose...if the specialist cannot dissuade him. For the irony is that the processes of specialist thinking threaten to deny the validity of philosophical thought altogether.

By the findings of the first specialists, scholars and thinkers were to be shocked and startled into a completely new way of thinking. Sadly, they were trained in error for all methods and philosophies which are evolved by material maxims alone cannot lead to the perception of the true value or significance of the facts they uncover.

Why? Because such methods and philosophies confuse fact with existence, and substance with reality. To the materialistic mind, fact and existence, substance and reality are one in the same thing. Such methods therefore limit what we can know, and how we can know. Such logic concludes that what is not factual and measurable does not exist.

If it is true, then the philosopher, the Spiritualist and the man who believes he is more than a collection of chemicals, is each in his turn silenced. And the seance of life in which we all participate with such hope and enthusiasm becomes nothing more than the relaying of endless facts.

If a sitter was only given an exhaustive list of facts about one departed individual, would he not be justified in replying with a shrug of the shoulders and a "So what?" But if the medium continues with, "This is your mother," all the facts are drawn together and become meaningful. If the medium adds something like, "She wants you to know that she is all right, and that there is life after death," then all the details at once become gloriously significant. The sitter learns something of life beyond his senses, and (on reflection) also learns more about himself: he is not his physical body, he is at present merely in a physical body.

We have learned from the rules of the seance room before.

Can we do so again? Has the specialist approach destroyed the significance man looks for or has it merely overlooked it?

Let us take a deeper look into this question of fact and knowledge so we may more fully appreciate the dilemma of the specialist who searches for the truth.

Over there is a bridge. The bridge, you say, is a fact. This conclusion is arrived at because the bridge exists physically. But the existing bridge is made up of bricks, stone, wood and metal. What is the absolute fact here? The one unalterable, permanent reality of the bridge is not the materials of the original bridge. These you can destroy; these you can grind and crush into the dust upon which you tread.

But you cannot alter in any way whatever the mathematical law which made such a feat of engineering possible. The law — the essence of a thing — is what does not change. The law — the essence of a thing — is real. The essence does not exist physically, does not have substance, but is just as I am.

Over there is a tree. The tree exists and so we say the tree is a fact. But why is the tree a fact? Because of the earth, the sun, the air, the rain. All these are facts. All exist. But the essence of the reality of a tree is not an existing tree, not the earth, sun, air or rain, but the law of growth. The law of growth does not exist physically, does not have substance. But it is real. It is.

The role of the specialist, in time, becomes absurd. As facts are split up and divided, then again subdivided, the specialist finds himself knowing more and more about less and less. Besides this, so much time is spent in search of, and examination of, the facts, that there is too little time left to meditate upon the true function and significance of the knowledge gathered.

We looked at Aristotle before, and remarked how his progress was hindered by the lack of appropriate equipment. The same could be said of the specialist who has made great strides in the collection of data, but has not the equipment to draw it together and discover its significance. What he lacks is the acceptance of the higher knowledge of true communion. He has not yet accepted that the essence of a thing is its reality; he has never fully grasped that physical existence is only a reflection of that reality.

Man can only ever know, can only ever hope to know the

essence of a thing for it is impossible for him to know all the facts about every physical example of it. And if once he knows the principle relating to the essence, then he can understand any "reflection" of it that he meets in his experience.

So it is that the philosopher emerges to act in a liaison capacity between the people and the specialist. It is the philosopher who tries to explain what all the facts are getting at.

The scientific approach of the specialist is by the path of pure intellect. Pure intellect is not concerned with human emotion, is unmoved by the voice of passion. Its only desire must be to know.

In contrast, the philosopher is fully aware of the confused yearnings and desires of the human family. He knows the painful dramas of frustrated passion and conflicting emotions soured in the dark world of ours; of ignorance; of the piteous, pleading entreaty of a society helplessly entrapped in the cruel shambles of power politics.

All these dramas move the heart and the perceiving mind of the philosopher to what I call his Divine Chemistry. He recognises that the findings of science must be selected and blended into a teaching, into a way of life. He sees that these fragments of knowledge have to be woven with inspired skill and vision into an intelligent theme. People need to know where they are going: they need to know their lives have meaning.

The Fatherhood of God is the very root of all true philosophy. If you don't like that phrase, start with "The one-ness of all life" or, as the poet would say, "One law, one God, one element and one far off divine event to which the whole creation moves."

To this one source, this one absolute, this one law, the philosopher must relate all fragments of life and knowledge, however varied in kind or character.

In their tasks, philosopher and scientist become something like Holmes and Watson. The scientist Watson examines the world carefully and discovers clues. The philosopher Holmes studies the clues to solve the problem and crack the case.

How does the philosopher set about tracking down the truth? There are two ways. The first is by plodding and hard graft: he looks at all the evidence, thinks hard about it, and gradually works out a pattern or series of consequences which are soundly based on

24

logic. Through this method, knowledge is slowly arrived at with a degree of mathematical exactness.

The second method is what detective story writers would call a hunch. Philosophers, with their liking for longer words and phrases, would probably call it inspiration, transcendental knowledge, spontaneous knowledge, even divine revelation.

The fact is that the answer comes with such intensity and certainty that it is often described in terms of religious experience because no other language can express it well enough. When the philosopher knows the answer in this way, he is knowing with the totality of his being. That is what I call "Communion".

Within the make-up of the dedicated men of science and philosophy, there exists some degree of the mystic, as patiently they proceed along the slow, plodding, rewarding path of endless experiments and ceaseless observations. The poet within each of them knows that somewhere in time is a moment when the solution to their problems will be revealed, when fragments of some higher knowledge will give to these searching, eager minds, an understanding of their knowledge.

I must make clear that this higher form of communion is no special free gift. There is no summer or winter sale at which we may purchase transcendental knowledge or divine revelation at bargain prices. No amount of ceremonial or ritual, chanting, drug-taking or being holy will provide a short cut to its attainment.

Only religion which has grown naturally out of the knowledge of science and philosophy can help us to understand the laws of this higher knowledge. From a religion which understands that all laws are natural — that nature all around us can teach us all things — from such a religion there will from time to time emerge the true mystic.

The life of such a mystic is both laborious and exacting. It is a life of one dedicated to the understanding of truth. There must be moments of long, careful meditation, moments of intense concentration. This is only possible when there is a sufficiency of pure desire: desire untainted by lust for success, fame or fortune, unsullied by ego-driven passion.

The desire of the mystic to know and to understand must be of such a burning intensity that it seems as if his very soul becomes scorched and blistered. The mystic never deliberately seeks the moment of divine revelation. He knows that moment is now, in the eternal present. The revelation occurs not in a particular place, but here, in that same eternal present.

Mental and spiritual exercise must open the eyes and make the mind clear so it may see and understand. Then, not all the while, when the mystic is himself attuned, when his being blends with all that is, he momentarily glimpses eternal truth and knows with a certainty beyond the knowing of his science and philosophy, all that he is capable of knowing at that point, whether his ability is in religion, art, science or whatever.

I would define such a true mystic as a highly trained, spiritual medium; for he too reaches out and returns with a message, so to speak. You see, there is an important distinction between what we might call an ordinary medium and a spiritual medium.

Ordinary mediumship is that which, first of all, is the important link between the people of the earth and the spirit worlds. Its most important function is to provide evidence for the seeker and to comfort the bereaved.

Now the spiritual medium does not have to concern himself with seeking evidence or obtaining special proof or signs. He can reach forth to higher levels and enjoy the joyous state of unfettered communion of soul with soul. The true mystic never deliberately or directly seeks this higher communion any more than an ordinary medium seeks to make contact with one specific personality. In both cases, the result depends largely on the openness and awareness of the medium at the time.

In man's quest to know, science and philosophy were evolved to help solve some of the many problems of the human family. There were the problems of how to obtain special food or sufficient food for all men; of providing all with adequate clothing, shelter and proper education; of conquering fear of pain and disease; of establishing successful forms of leadership and government for a population ever growing in number and complexity. These were just some of the more urgent problems which science and philosophy were resolved to deal with.

Science and philosophy have made enough knowledge available to men to solve most of humanity's more urgent needs. The

26

great tragedy of the human family is that despite the tremendous achievements of our intellectuals, many of the problems they first set out to solve are with us still. As far as I can see, there are three main reasons for this.

Firstly, as we sought to know more and more, the stress was gradually placed on the importance of education. This in turn caused a most significant change to occur in the human make-up. As the mind or intellect enters into its own more and more, so less and less does man make use of instinct and intuition. Up to this point, both of these faculties had been very powerful, but with the increasing emphasis on formal education, these two human powers of instinct and intuition became blunted through lack of use.

How often have we seen sick people be allowed to die through too much science and too little intuition? Have we not many times seen the intuition of a caring friend or helper succeed where medical science had failed?

The same thing is, of course, true of other sciences, as ecologists today so often point out. This often results in ordinary people regarding science with some mistrust, but this is well-founded in the sense that science is only part of the approach to understanding, not the entire approach. In itself it is excellent because it provides facts, but our use of it is sometimes at fault as we do not take the time to see the significance of those facts.

When it is understood that knowledge of psychic law is as important as any other form of knowledge, and when we realise that the psychic faculties of instinct and intuition need to be cultivated and developed in tandem with the intellect, then a major part of the human battle to know will be won.

A second reason for many of man's problems staying unsolved is language. Quite apart from the obvious complications of having so many different spoken languages — each with their own idiomatic usage — there is the difficulty we all have in expressing our thoughts and feelings clearly in words.

Quite often when a scientist has to make a statement about some newly acquired knowledge, his use of words is so strange and complex that only his closest associates could have any idea of what he is talking about.

Look at quantum physics and the language there: their use of the word "colour" as applied to force has nothing to do with the rainbow spectrum you or I might think of. And what do they mean by quarks or fractals? We can learn if we make the effort, but in the meanwhile, much of the language of new science tells us more about our own ignorance than anything else.

Even in everyday conversation there are continual slips and inaccuracies. The words spoken rarely express exactly what the mind intends to convey. A medium may say, "I see a tall gentleman here," yet it is more than likely he does not see this with his eyes, and, in fact, may not even have a visual impression of the man. No wonder some in the audience are confused about mediumship.

A government may encourage "individual enterprise," but whereas this might mean freedom to earn for one listener, it may mean the disbanding of a social service to another. In so many cases, where there is communication there is also confusion.

This leads us to a further disadvantage of the spoken or written word. Sometimes words are used apparently to communicate, but their effect is to obscure and confuse. Jargon is meaningful to its own coterie, but to a layman or outsider, it remains a mystery.

Legal terminology is one example where the common man needs to pay the professional to "interpret" for him. Many a professional consultant is paid to guide us through the morass of communication in every field of knowledge. Of course it remains in their financial interest to maintain that morass, their own knowledge of it, and our ignorance. "One great use of words," said Voltaire, "is to hide our thoughts."

It is this inclination to keep ideas to ourselves, to deceive, this lack of honesty among men, that results in the devaluation of the spoken word. Yet as with the mistrust of science, it is not the science just as it is not the words which are to be questioned, but man's use of them.

In our use of knowledge and our expression of it, there is an absolute need to be as simple, clear and honest as possible. The problem is that we are not. We have reached the third reason for man's lack of progress: his morality.

All philosophers, world teachers, poets and visionaries have in their turn dealt with this problem, but man's confusion is ever increased. There were high hopes that education would bring about the desired moral standard, but alas, education itself is unable to cope with the weakness of the nature of the human being. Indeed, it is felt that for the time being at any rate, we could do with a little less greatness and rather more goodness.

But what is good? This is a most difficult question to answer since everything can, at the same moment, be good, bad and indifferent. Music can be good to the appreciative listener, bad to the unappreciative and indifferent to the deaf. Before we can go any further, we have to ask if there is anything in life which is good and can never be anything else but good.

The answer is "Yes." It is not a fact, not a thing or example, nothing with substance. What is good is the essence of life itself. You can call it the law of God if you like. That is unchangingly good.

How can we go about living according to the essence of life? We can look for the natural laws affecting our being.

Can we find these laws by the virtue of pure reason? That sounds feasible, because when we live by pure reason, it seems we can only be and do that which is right, that which is good.

"Fine," you say. But wait a minute, for it is here that the whole case of our thinking breaks down. Why? Because pure reason is defeated, dethroned and overpowered, by emotion. We no sooner construct a moral system than another aspect of ourselves overturns it.

Are we so much at war with ourselves — head against heart — that we are doomed to make no progress at all? Surely the answer cannot be "Yes."

The answer is not "Yes" because there is more to us than heart and head: we are spirit too, and it is the inheritance of our spiritual nature that we have the ability of communion. If we recognise this ability in ourselves, we can nurture it until we grow into that inheritance and actively commune with the very essence of life itself and participate in that very special kind of knowing. Herein lies the kernel of our morality.

Spiritual communion is the basis of complete life because it deals with the complete man. The world can become one vast seance room in which the turbulent emotions of men become mellowed. Being at last brought into association with their spiritual counterparts, inhaling the rich spiritual air generated by communion at this high level in a manner holy and sacred, men can become eternally intertwined with the true essence of the complete self. Then they shall know. Let spiritual Communion determine morality.

No man who has breathed into his soul the breath of celestial air can ever be anything but good. And since goodness is the essence of life, all else will in due course recede in the breathless hush of such communion: private desires will be merged into the universal order.

The greatest good is in a sense illusory. In communion we realise we are parts of the infinite flow of essence, of law, of God. That flow fills us with being greater than our petty selves and timeless beyond our petty life-span. Our human existence is nothing more than an incident in the drama of life, a fitful flash in an eternal night.

When self is merged with the greater self, there shines from the human breast a light as warm, as holy, as ever shone from the hills of Galilee. Then of life, its experience and its purpose man can say not only, "I am," but "I know," and his inner being will once again be defined in words similar to these:

"The intelligent being in man, whose form is light, whose thoughts are true, whose nature is like ether and from whom all works, all desires, all sweet odours and tastes proceed, who never speaks and is never surprised, he is myself within my heart.

"Smaller than a corn of rice, smaller than a grain of mustard seed, he is also myself within the heart. Greater than the earth, greater than the heavens, greater than all these worlds."

Communion with the Divine Spirit is the ultimate aim of Spiritualism.

Chapter 3

FIRST FRUITS

TAKING the first faltering steps is the only way to achieve even the grandest purpose.

I took my first service while I was still 14. We had moved from Yew Street, and had a room to meet in over The Crown. Word got round about the message I had given Mrs Thomas so when one of our booked speakers didn't turn up, Mrs Isaacs (the president) wondering who could take the service, looked round and said, "Oh, Billy can take it!" It was a joke, of course, but at the time I didn't realise it.

"Yes," I said, "I'll take it." It wasn't until I was sitting next to her on the platform that I realised what I had done. I looked at the congregation and was terrified! However, I just opened my mouth, the words came...and I got on fine.

A couple of weeks later, much to my surprise, I was told that I was booked to take the service at Treherbert. In order to get there, I had to go early to work to ask to be allowed out to catch the bus. Usually, because the walk to the pit was so long, we used to stop off at points along the way and sit and chat. That day, I kept on walking so that I would arrive promptly, before my boss, David Templeman. That I did.

"Good morning, Billy, you're early today," he said, before I began to strip off and get ready for work. Later in the day, I approached him again, and asked — on account of my being early — if I could leave at the proper stopping time in order to catch the bus to Treherbert. You see, we never stopped exactly at stopping time. Sometimes it would be thirty minutes or three quarters of an hour later when we finished the section we were on. He agreed to let me out with the harriers who always stopped on time.

By and by, through the rest of the day, when he saw me, he would exchange a few words until he learned that I wanted to go to the church there - not to hear a speaker or have a tea, but to take the service. Mr Templeman worked out that, as it was a weekday meeting, there would be more than just a speaker there. "So, you are a medium then?" he asked. Being used to the kind of banter the admission of being a Spiritualist would generate, I admitted cautiously that I was. To my surprise, he was very interested, for he, too, was a Spiritualist from Cefn Hengoed, ten miles away.

"If you are a medium then," he said, "I wonder if you could do me a favour."

"I'll try," I said. "What is it?"

"Well, I have family in Australia," he explained. "Over the years, we've lost touch. I wonder if you can find out how they are for me?" I said I would do my best, and in the weeks that followed, would try and find something out for him. On my first attempt, I drew a blank. I could get nothing at all. When next he asked me, I told him I had received nothing. Three weeks later, he asked again. Again I had drawn a blank and told him so.

On his third enquiry, I had to apologise for my lack of success.

Due to pit closures, it wasn't until some eight years later that I next met him, this time at an open air meeting. He didn't recognise me at first, but when he did, Mr Templeman explained to his friend I was the best boy he had ever had, and that I was a real medium.

"What makes you say that?" I asked.

"You passed the test," he said, taking me back to the time of the favour he asked of me.

"You made up nothing," he said. "You just gave what you got, and you were right! You see, I have no family in Australia." I had gained his respect, because even at the third enquiry, I made up nothing to please him. It was a good lesson to learn...even if it was a long time in coming.

It is always best to do whatever you do as well as you can. In time, you will gain true recognition for that, and that will make up for the occasions you are snubbed and overlooked.

W. H. Evans was a famous writer, speaker and demonstrator in my youth. When I was still 14, I met him. He was at the railway station, waiting to go to Tonypandy to take a service, while I was travelling to Treharris for the same reason.

I had stepped into a compartment where a small, rather shabbily dressed man was sitting in the corner. I must admit, I felt rather sorry for him. At the end of the journey, however, the secretary of Trealaw church met us coming out of the train and introduced us. On the return journey, Mr and Mrs Alexander, Spiritualists from Penarth, met up with us. Mrs Alexander asked me where I had been. "What were you doing there?" asked she.

"Why, taking the service," I replied.

"I suppose you know all about it?" she went on.

"No," was my earnest answer. "Do you?"

It was not intended to be impertinent, but I don't think she quite knew what to say.

W. H. Evans smiled and broke the silence with, "I think he can take care of himself very well!" He continued, "May I give you some advice?" I nodded because I was keen to learn, particularly from such a well informed man.

"Wherever you go and take a service, people will congratulate you and make a fuss of you. Not necessarily for the quality of your work, but because you are a young lad. Later, when you're older like me, you have to earn their respect."

It was a useful piece of advice to be given — and I remembered it well.

Now, although thanks and praise may be thinner on the ground, I think I know when I am truly appreciated, so the outer demonstrations of approval are less important than they were in my youth.

When steady work was difficult to get, my father found employment in Birmingham, round about 1929. This meant he could only come home once a month, so at sixteen years old, I was left in charge of my father's three cherished allotments.

Victor Ford was quite a strict man who didn't express his feelings freely. However, with the help of friends on neighbouring allotments, I learnt the skills of gardening, and must have made at least a passable job, for although my father was non-committal, he seemed pleased with the work.

It was then that I began to realise how much Nature could teach, if you would only take the time to observe her carefully.

Chapter Four

NATURAL PHILOSOPHY

COME out and see the garden. It's not very big, but there's always lots of work to do. Down here on the slabs are the fuchsias. Oh, I know, there's nothing much to see just now. Just a stalk and a few green leaves. But they'll come. With care and attention, they'll come.

Up there you can see the patch I was telling you about. I've dug and double dug that until the earth is as fine as silk. It drifts through your fingers. See? And there's not a trace of anything anywhere. The seeds are planted - newly planted - so there's nothing to see...except the care I've taken.

If nothing at all happens to this patch to break its brown perfection, if it stays exactly as it is now, forever, then perfect though it is, it would be dead. I'm a gardener. I'm interested in excellence, not perfection; in life, not death. Come again in a month or so and the brown will be relieved by the green of the young sprouts poking through.

By the summer you'll see the soft fern of the carrot tops, the fleshy-leaved potato plants, the gaudy orange flowers of the runner beans. You'll see the change. And by September the foliage will give way to fruit. Another month and I'll be clearing away and getting started all over again.

The joy of gardening is the joy of watching changes unfold before your eyes.

Now where there is change, there is life. Growth, the manifestation of life, is change. Needless to say, all the natural world is teeming with life. We recognise that life because things move: they change their appearance, their sound, their smell and so on. My philosophy is one of change and growth. I call it natural philosophy because I am interested in excellence, not perfection; in life, not death.

My philosophy has the label of Spiritualism, although that in itself may change because all living things do. For the moment, the word Spiritualism suits very well. "Spirit" means life — and life is the most natural thing in the world. Spiritualism is natural philosophy. It is an approach to living which says that the changing life in a body is much more important than the body itself.

But if I am to make myself clear, maybe I should start from where so many people are today. My philosophy is not one that is popularly held. That is not surprising really when those in employment spend most of their time and effort earning money to spend on things.

In a society like ours, it is easy to slip into the mistake of thinking that physical things are valuable. We are seen to be successful when we have gathered around us all the consumer items you can imagine — car, house, works of art, clothes, food — anything you can buy. Of course, each of these brings its own pleasures, but if you think about it, there is no pleasure in them unless you use them. It is you who give them value.

If I put that another way, you might see things differently: it is you who are valuable, not the things you own. You make those things sources of pleasure. When you tire of them, they no longer are pleasurable and so "lose" their value. They have not changed, but you have. And you have changed because you are alive while your car, house, foreign holiday or whatever, do not live.

If you are like me, you will find the things you value most are not physical ones. Materialism will not satisfy you. It will not satisfy you because you are alive and you change: material things do not live, do not change.

Furthermore, if you are looking for some ground rules on how best to live your life, a changeless philosophy (one that is totally abstract and unchanging) may not suit you. But natural philosophy might, simply because it grows with you and is a philosophy based on life and living.

Spiritualism is a religion which concentrates on the ever-changing spirit of the individual. It does not say, "One day you will be perfect." Instead it teaches that even beyond the death of your physical body, your spirit will continue to evolve eternally. It implies that even God is constantly evolving, for surely He (or She, or It) is also alive and therefore changing.

Spiritualism tells you, "You are not your body," as materialists would suggest. "You are merely in your body." The essential you is the life, the spirit, within that body.

As a religion, Spiritualism is saying that the way to God is through tending your spirit. The first stage is to become aware of it. In a way, it is saying the most important things in a garden are the changes that happen in it, not the square yards of earth that it is made up of. What is important is how you use that earth to allow the changes of flower and fruit and growth to occur.

Now, if we continue the metaphor, natural philosophy is like the gardener's manual instructing you how best to prepare the soil and tend the plants so as to maximise growth. Let's take a look at the contents page then.

1. Environment: all life is subject to atmosphere and environ ment.

2. Two-fold law: creativity works through opposites

3. Association: any kind of growth or development requires association

4. Involve to evolve: energy has to be absorbed before it can be transmuted to a higher form

5. Sequence: there is a natural sequence to all growth.

You can call them chapter headings if you like, or spiritual laws if that appeals to you. In my experience, they are principles which apply to the physical and spiritual growth alike. In applying these principles carefully and thoughtfully, growth—both physical and spiritual — occurs. They are the natural laws of a natural philosophy. I shall take them one at a time.

ENVIRONMENT

All life is subject to atmosphere and environment. We are much more aware of the significance of our environment today than we were thirty years ago when I first talked about this subject.

Now we know if we take away the hedgerows, we not only divest the countryside of its beauty, but lose the wild life which fed on the pests which eat our crops away. If we do not maintain the correct environment we create an imbalance which, in turn, generates more and more problems. The greenhouse effect is a worldwide problem, hedgerows a local one, but atmosphere affects small groups, individuals and attitudes too.

Any change in atmosphere is immediately reflected by alterations in all forms of life which exist in that atmosphere. For example, when the temperature drops, water always freezes, the growth of plants stops and animal life is reduced to a minimum.

In the human kingdom, cold makes the thought less free, imagination becomes dull, and emotions are less alert and alive. Coldness in human behaviour retards the natural development and unfoldment of affection, friendship and love, and makes them clumsy and awkward.

Cold may be nothing more than atmosphere, but it can have a very powerful effect all the same. Think of the cynic who approaches the developing medium: he seems to shrivel up what gift she may have. Coldness in our approach to the spiritual universe freezes psychic energy, dimming the power of perception. It is only an attitude, an atmosphere, but, oh, what a difference it makes!

It can mean the difference between desolation and jubilation. Think of warmth. All life becomes sensitive and alert to any increase in warmth or heat from the atmosphere. The whole of nature will respond to the warmth of a new day. All life bestirs itself to acknowledge that gentle, coaxing, entreating, encouraging voice of warmth and heat. Our souls rejoice in the warmth of love, and blossom into generosity, altruism or the brightness of laughter.

Atmosphere and environment will determine whether we grow, and at what rate we grow. If we make this truth our own, and make it work, we can control the environment of our lives physically, emotionally, mentally and spiritually to grow and to develop.

TWO-FOLD LAW

Creativity works through opposites. Cold and heat (whether we are referring to the thermometer's measurement or the openness/closedness of a relationship) are at different ends of the spectrum.

There are many others: night and day, ebb and flow, sleep and awareness, male and female, inertia and activity. If not opposites, they are certainly at extremes. If life is to unfold, it requires the right atmosphere, but it also needs to have close and intimate contact with these other extremes or opposite states/forms of life.

This brings us to the second law. Creativity arises through the association of opposites. Life is change. Change is a movement towards something different from the present state. The process of such change is creativity. This creativity happens when, in some way, B evolves towards its opposite A.

Political systems move from one brand of dictatorship towards liberalism. When that is achieved, liberalism drifts towards dictatorship once more. The second dictatorship will not be identical to the first, but significantly different in some ways.

We begin to see that the circular movement of creativity or evolution is in fact a spiral, moving round and up at the same time. But the movement of change is from one thing to its opposite, and we learn on the way, if we are fortunate. The form of a seed expands into a plant, and the plant contracts when it ceases to function. Once again we see the cycle of creativity, this time in nature. Creativity is the association of opposites.

ASSOCIATION

Association of life with life is imperative for the development of power. New sources of energy are continually being made available to man as a result of one substance being blended with another, of one energy affecting another. Contact has to be made.

"No man is an island entire of itself" is just as true of any other living thing you may mention. All life is the constant dance of one thing coming into contact with another: sometimes to no avail, sometimes to react intensely.

The farmer, the scientist, the engineer, the physician: all play their full part in the story of evolution by endless experiment in this direction. They follow the lesson nature teaches by continually bringing another two together. In the same way, the wise philosopher brings two unlike ideas together and works his way to a new conclusion. And in the name of love, caring and friendship, we, throughout our lives, make contact with others. So we grow too.

Sex energy can only find its true outlet by association with the opposite sex : mate calls to mate. Friend reaches forth to friend; soul yearns for affinity with soul. Whatever else we learn from our passage through life, we shall understand through our own experience, the need for others — other people, other things, other ideas. And through this we learn of our relationship to all life. We cannot grow alone.

INVOLVE TO EVOLVE

Nor can we grow along with all the variety the world has to offer unless there is some exchange between us and the world. If we remain untouched physically or emotionally, or mentally or spiritually, then that "other" has not truly existed for us. For there to be growth, there has to be a transfer of energy of some sort.

The basic laws of breathing and eating illustrate this clearly. In breathing we inhale air, a mixture of oxygen, nitrogen and carbon dioxide.

We use the oxygen we extract to refresh and enliven all parts of our body, then exhale a higher percentage of carbon dioxide. We have in effect drawn off or transferred the life-giving properties from the air to ourselves. Thus we sustain our own living systems.

In eating we digest the food and draw the nutrients from it to build and maintain our bodies. But the transfer of energy does not stop there. We may use the energy of our bodies in many ways. We "transfer" it during any activity you care to name. By tidying the house we create order, by speaking to a neighbour we generate pleasure, by cuddling a child we make him feel secure.

Each of life's acts is a transfer of energy. And if another person is aware of that act, it will leave a mental as well as a physical impression.

The life-giving principle, through all its many kingdoms, constantly transfers its energy from one form to another. This life force, this energy, is continually being redirected to manifest its power in new and different paths, new and different ways. Nature is at work constantly rearranging and watching the effect.

It is through this process that character, distinction, separateness evolve. The culture of every society truly reflects the association it has had with other forms of life. A man's personality is the sum total of his reactions to his life's experiences. But remember, it is NOT the total of his experiences, it is the total of his REACTIONS. The energy that flowed from him is what is significant.

Let's look at the process so far. First we associate with, link or juxtapose one thing with another. Then there is a reaction between the two, a transfer of energy. As a result of this transference, both things are changed. Through this change, growth may occur. When such a change is happening due to a planned arrangement, we have what we call creativity.

This has always been regarded as an intensely personal thing. The artist insists he is expressing himself, the scientist describes his search for a solution. When we describe the process as one of "blood, sweat and tears," we are taking of physical, emotional and intellectual involvement. Such involvement allows a transference of energy at a personal level.

It is as if you have literally to give of yourself if you wish to receive your answer, inspiration, solution, invention or whatever. In this way you grow: you involve to evolve, so to speak. You have to transmit to transmute; or in the words of the Master, you have to lose the world if you want to gain the world.

SEQUENCE

But you have to do it in the right order. When you look at nature, you are inevitably struck by its regularity. Look at the way leaves grow on a stem, or how petals unfold; how day follows night, and summer, spring. A child leans to crawl, walk and then run. There is always a sequence to growth. There is always a dependability in nature's laws.

In fact, if it was not for this regularity and dependability, we could know very little. As it is, this sequential order of the universe gently leads man to new expectations, fresh hope and faith that by keen observation and careful reasoning, he could extend what he has learned from the physical life in nature beyond those restrictions into the mental and spiritual.

This extrapolation allows man to speculate with ideas, ideas on which science has no comment or advice to offer. Development has a natural sequence.

Well now, we have glimpsed through the "Gardener's manual" and gained a rough impression of the principles we are expected to put into action. But no gardener will have confidence in a mere book unless its contents reflect (at least to some extent) his own practical experience. We are gardeners of the spirit. Let us ask two questions:

How do these principles relate to our own experience of spiritual development in man?

If they relate well, how can we continue to promote that spiritual growth?

I suppose that since man's consciousness first stirred, he has thought about his future and felt the need to know there was more to life than meets his senses.

If that were not so, the Hydesville Rappings with their tediously spelled out message from the deceased Charles B. Rosna would soon have been relegated to the oblivion of the world's curiosities. But look at when they happened, and you will see the significance of the sequence we were talking about. They occurred in1848.

Look at where they occurred and you will realise the importance of the atmosphere : in a Quaker community.

Just as surely as a chick breaks out of its shell when there is nothing more there of sustain it, so human consciousness broke through the restriction of the five senses to reach out for what it — consciously or subconsciously — needed for its well-being. Both in Northern America and Great Britain, the Industrial Revolution was well established by 1848, bringing with it its consumerism and materialism. Soon its religious foundations were to be rocked by Darwin, but in the meanwhile, the needs of the physical man were being catered for at the expense of the spiritual man. Something had to give. It did.

In a community strongly influenced by Quakers who still made a point of listening to their own stillness, the poltergeist phenomena enabled by the two adolescent Fox sisters formed the first crude channel of mediumship through which Spirit could once again touch the hearts and minds of human beings in the mid-nineteenth century.

The time and environment were both just right to stimulate a major change in the religious outlook of the country so the "craze" of Spiritualism swept the American continent for the next twenty years or so.

We are left a century later to pick out the gems amidst the dust of hysteria, fraud, showmanship and wishful thinking.

But somewhere amidst all the confusion, the most advanced thinkers of the age gave their verdicts on this philosophy which had sprung from the new phenomena of Spiritualism. These verdicts served to intensify man's instinctive desire to reach out for an understanding of life which would reveal to him the possibility of a way of life which would be both right and just, a way of life that would grow and develop with him.

To the clear seeing eye and feeling heart, it seemed not only unnatural, wrong and evil that the religious teachings of the day confused more than they instructed and enlightened. It seemed unnatural and wrong that the theological doctrines were much more concerned with correct observance of creed and ritual than with natural compassion. Why should the teachings concern a permanent state rather than a continuing growth and evolution?

Throughout this century, the orthodox church has made many moves towards involvement and compassion, but there are still churchmen today whose concern over the doctrines of the Virgin Birth or the physical resurrection of Christ only encourages people to turn their backs on a religion such as this.

Is it any wonder that secular organisations like the World Wildlife Fund or Greenpeace have emerged as society's channels for caring, when what they do is seen to be done, and nature's delicate balance is slowly restored? Natural compassion has been released more effectively by the media than many religious leaders.

Through the last couple of centuries, man has evolved sufficiently to master the physical stuff of his world. The reward within our own society has been a higher standard of living and many more physical comforts. The price has been all the problems of a materialistic outlook.

Man's growth is now towards the opposite of this material-ism —if our manual is correct — towards the spiritual, towards natural philosophy. This would seem to be the point we have arrived at in our growth. But what of the atmosphere? Is it right for growth?

The soil of poverty and ignorance is not the natural soil that nurtures evolving life which always yearns for the fuller, wider unfoldment of the spirit within. Poverty and ignorance of the past were often the result of deliberate and calculated efforts to suppress knowledge.

Political, industrial and religious rulers all too often regarded humanity as just so many bodies - bodies they would not hesitate to trample upon if it meant they could proceed with their own onward, forward march towards their own self-satisfaction.

In some cases, it is still the same today, but poverty isn't always the lack of food and shelter any more than ignorance is restricted to the uneducated. The richest man is poor when he cannot trust his friends to love him for himself alone. We are poor when we lack what we need to survive and grow, whether that lack is fresh air, peace and quiet, friendship or food.

The cleverest man is ignorant when he has lost his way in life, doesn't know he has a soul or can't understand how to give love to another. And today we are so busy earning, getting ahead, spending, innovating and cramming each day with frenetic activity that we are living examples of the propaganda which prolongs the existence of poverty and ignorance in the name of prosperity and knowledge. The effect is to crush all growing from the spirit. The result is sickness and ill health, both personal and social.

Well, if materialism isn't making us healthy, wealthy and wise, can Spiritualism with its natural philosophy do any better? Remember we are talking about a body of thought which says that it is the life in the thing which is important, not the thing itself. It is therefore easy to see what Emerson meant when he said, "Nature is divine - a screen, the glory of the One breaks through everywhere."

It is life — or God — which flickers through each object to us if we allow ourselves to see it there. This demonstration of wholeness which nature displays to us should be the beginning of the wisdom or understanding we seek. And when we know that we, too, are part of this glorious unity, we cannot be poor. Such an attitude provides the right atmosphere for our spirits to grow.

Chapter Five

INTO SERVICE

BY my late teens, I was involved in the church committee and its work, raising matters for discussion when others were reluctant to. However, there was one meeting I didn't attend. It was the one where they were trying to decide who should run the Lyceum. The Lyceum was really the Spiritualist equivalent of the Sunday School. It was designed to educate children and adults in healthy living, self-expression, Spiritualist principles and teachings.

True to many a church committee meeting, there was long and heated discussion as to who should take over. I don't know all the ins and outs of the discussion, but the responsibility became mine ...by just one vote.

It was a challenge which I met wholeheartedly, and led eventually to my being President of the South Wales Lyceum Union. It was a pleasure to see, during the term of my Presidency, the number of Lyceums in South Wales increase from two to twelve. The movement was strong in those days, and supported annual competitions for the best Lyceum in the Union.

But when I first became involved in New Street's Lyceum, the major challenge each year was an anniversary celebration when the Lyceum would offer a programme of readings and music. The first year I took over, the hall was only about a third full: it had to be improved!

As a bandsman, I have always had a great love of music, so it was with great enthusiasm that the Lyceum workers and I put together a programme of music to be sung by the young people's choir. Our joint enthusiasm must have been infectious because twice the usual number of children turned up to be in the choir.

Word spread until so many of an audience appeared for the performance that we couldn't get them all in! Mrs Davis, presiding on the Sunday, was delighted to announce that the programme would be repeated on the Monday evening at seven to make sure everyone would finally get a seat. We went from strength to strength.

Enthusiasm bred more enthusiasm. I had a friend who kept "The Angel" pub. He had a splendid tenor voice, and volunteered to sing for us. Another friend, Marsden, and I sang a duet, and so it went on until yes, our Lyceum could produce a success worthy of any Mount Zion!

I could only have been eighteen when I was busy looking out music at church one night. Some of our members, Mr and Mrs Mason, Mrs Isaacs and John Thomas, were deep in discussion about a problem. "Well, why not ask Willie as he's our minister," said Mrs Isaacs. That's when I first felt like a minister. It's true I was asked to become a Minister of the Spiritualists' National Union in the forties, but no award makes a minister. If the people think of you as their minister, then you are.

I suppose there are times in everyone's life when they are keen to become involved in spiritual work, but never seem to get the opportunity to do what they think they could do well. That has happened to me, but "When the time is right, you will be asked to work. The work will come to you." So I was told — and so it came to be.

One distraught mother wanted a Spiritualist funeral for her son, who had been in my Lyceum. The nearest official minister was A. W. Harris from Treharris, but that was too far away. The alternative was Mr Thorne, but he was unable to take the service at the arranged time. As a result, I was asked to take my first funeral.

It didn't worry me to take on such a responsibility. I knew I could do it. Funerals were quite a thing in those days, with the coffin held aloft, and the procession behind it. I took the book with the Order of Service in it, but then, as now, I did not stick to it. Each person is different. The words we speak have to be specially for them to make it their service. For me, that is the way it has to be.

Once the people had witnessed my service, they no longer

asked for ministers out of the village. From then on I took many such services, always carrying the formal handbook, but never using the format!

It often upset my mother that because my father was unemployed, I was not able even to go to grammar school. I couldn't have cared less. I did what work was asked of me, and just got on with it. Perhaps there is too much store set on certificates and the like. No certificate can ever make you a healer, minister or medium. To do those things, you have to care. You have to feel. That has nothing to do with certificates.

I had discussed the responsibilities of being a minister with my parents. At first they were worried about the comments others might make, but when these proved to be favourable, that problem solved itself. My parents were then quite happy for me to undertake the work. The main problem — and one that was never fully resolved — was that of finance.

I have always made it my principle never to charge for services, and only to take expenses...if they are offered! What Spirit gives is not for buying and selling. To ask for a fee is somehow demeaning. It lowers the work of Spirit.

Well, at that time, ministers received 4 shillings for a service. However, for me to take such a service, I had to lose a day's work. The minimum wage then was 8 or 9 shillings so when there was a funeral to take, I was without pocket money for the week!

I can't say I minded too much: the entertainment that week would be limited to a penny fish and a penny's worth of chips at Pesces — delicious!

My connection with Will Thomas — the lad saved by my first message — was not over. Some time after the incident at the pit, the Thomases moved, but when he was about twenty, Will was taken into Swansea asylum with no hope of him being released due to his disturbed mental state. His mother was naturally distraught, and contacted me for help because it seemed to her there was no other hope. I sat with her for a while and told her not to worry, that within one month he would be all right.

I gathered together a healing group of friends: Will Mason, John Thomas, Mrs Thomas and Tom Fletcher. We agreed to sit and meditate for Will's healing as often as was possible. In consequence, our patient made definite progress. His mother was delighted because any improvement at all was so much more than specialists had thought possible. To our joy, Will was sent home — within the month, as predicted. He amazed his doctors with the progress he made. And they declared him fully fit on his departure.

Naturally Will Thomas and his family were sensitive about his experience in Swansea, and once again the family moved, this time to Birmingham. But when finally his mother ("Auntie Lizzie" to us) took ill and died, I took her funeral service at her request.

The superintendent of the crematorium there was highly unco-operative with, and sceptical of, Spiritualists, but after the service, I'm glad to say his attitude had changed completely.

It is only by living out the reality of our beliefs, effectively and in the public eye, that we can fully demonstrate to others what Spiritualism really is. It is so much more than just the platform mediumship many are familiar with. For that is just the beginning.

Chapter Six

NATURAL MEDIUMSHIP

NATURE—if we will but look —provides us with endless variety and instructs us to seek the life within it all. The towering hill, the winding valley, boundless sea and bright constellation, each with its silent voice declares the divinity of life, makes manifest a power and speaks of an order which declares itself natural.

A natural order of the universe appeals to the living soul of man. It touches and moves him until he feels he must evolve a way of life and a philosophy from the starting point: nature. His inner being demands a natural philosophy so he might understand life and share in its wealth.

I think the Hydesville Rappings of 1848 were just one attempt by Spirit to remind people of the wealth of nature, to tell them it is the life in the body which is significant, not the body itself. Today, every time a person communicates effectively through a medium to you or me, Spirit is saying the same thing : "Look - no body! But plenty of Life." Each of us has to learn this for himself, and having learned it, to look at everything in a different light.

The natural phenomena of both the psychic and spiritual order witnessed in the seances of early Spiritualists had two effects, pretty much as they do today. They proved to be highly intriguing and entertaining, which explains the rapid social success of Spiritualism before the turn of the century, and the fame of the occasional Spiritualist celebrity even today.

However, such a shallow, superficial effect could not — and does not—last. Fortunately, these same phenomena also stimulate intellectual enquiry among a few. Although scant attention is paid to their work today, eminent scientists of their time, like Sir William Crookes, Alfred Russell Wallace, Sir Oliver Lodge, William Barrett and others, researched painstakingly into the natural phenomena of mediumship.

Their subjects were very often quite ordinary, honest, simple people who were found to have a sensitivity beyond their physical senses. From the research of these scientists, the following three facts emerged:

1. There exists a spiritual universe.
2. Within this spiritual universe there are intelligent life forces which can communicate with earth life through mediumship.
3. Such communications have established that the human consciousness (still having a form, feeling and memory) survives physical death.

These scientists, through their own work, were satisfied that these facts were well established. But if they are to be significant to us, we have to ask: "What do they mean? How do they affect us?" The communications received from these intelligent life forces suggest that physical existence is nothing more than a phase in a wider life, just as adolescence or middle age are phases which we grow through in a wider span of years.

What we have received from Spirit suggests that life and its progress moves according to basic principles. It would be foolish to accept such information unquestioningly simply because it came from an unusual source. But because the information has come through man in a natural way, and the principles can be tested in the natural world, they are worthy of our consideration. Hence the "manual" at the beginning of the chapter.

It is easy to see we are subject to some kind of law, whatever that might be. It does not matter what our colour is, or our class, where we come from, what era we belong to, what age we are: if we go without food we shall feel hunger.

We shall always get tired when we refuse to rest, grow cold when there is no heat. We cannot avoid the unseen hand of time declaring the moment when we are no longer young. All of these very simple laws apply to our physical bodies. Sometimes we may try to fight or ignore them, but the results of these laws are inevitable. We are irrecoverably immersed in her environment where nature allows no favourites, expresses no sentiment. The way of her world is hard and rough.

But perhaps she knows that if she were to pamper us, she would hinder rather than help. Her January gales lop the trees and encourage a stronger growth in spring. We observe her and learn: we prune our roses and expect sturdy stems and many buds for our efforts. Not only this, we realise that the man who has suffered setbacks in his life grows into a stronger character, better able to withstand Fortune's "pruning" and even profit by it.

The simple rules of nature apply not only to our bodies, but to our minds and personalities too. They are multi-level, embodying the principles which are universal in their application.

Recognising these principles, how then can we improve our lives? I think we can do two things.

Firstly, we can promote a people-based, God-aspiring religion. Secondly, we can develop mediumship as the living practice of religion.

Religious thought should take for its raw material the life that is now; the life that is constantly manifesting itself in you and me and nature. It should be people-centred, not prose-centred. Its principles ought to be the principles of life.

To understand nature, man uses constant study, question-and-answer, observation and experiment. Surely to understand the non-physical of "supernature," he should try these same approaches before he abandons them for the alternatives of faith, superstition or textual analysis. Religious truth does not concern itself with specific times, places or people. That is the job of history. Religion deals with that which exists, but cannot be captured or measured; it deals with the life which is constantly changing and adapting; it deals with the essential nature of life and its ultimate purpose.

We accept that evolution is a physical process and continues through the psychological, the social, the cultural. We can trace the evolution of ideas; we are aware of the growth of feelings. All this is to the good, but we must not forget that evolution is a process of growth into the beyond: beyond what we are, what we feel, what we think. Evolution is a process of the spirit, too.

It might well be that evolution of the physical and mental

51

without the parallel growth of the spirit causes many of the symptoms we call sickness - individual and social. If there is too great a discrepancy, the physical, mental and spiritual system of man becomes unbalanced. There should be a natural binding together of these parts if he is to be and to feel whole. This is what any living religion should be able to do.

Mediumship is the act, the process, the very practice of religion. It is not empty theory, but living, subjective experience of the life of spirit: your own and other's.

The first great function of mediumship is to provide evidence as to the reality of a spiritual universe, peopled by those who once lived on this earth. That is not something you should have to take for granted. You should be able to prove it for yourself.

The natural sequence of this first function is to bring a closer association between the people of these two worlds. Nothing is more natural. It is nothing more than the continuation of a natural law of unfoldment. It is as much a reaching out to the beyond as any other evolutionary adventure. We can trace its course through every grade and realm of creation.

We have already looked at the law of breathing : it is the first principle of creative life. All forms of life are subject to this principle. Methods may differ. Degrees and levels may differ. But in the final analysis it is the same law : response to atmosphere.

You breathe in; you breathe out. Inhale to exhale. You involve to evolve; absorb to transmit. Life can only survive by feeding on life. Air absorbs water; water absorbs wood, iron, salt; vegetation absorbs air and water. Animal absorbs air, water, vegetation. And physical man absorbs all of these.

But the law applies to all man's levels, so mental man absorbs or breathes in by seeing, feeling and hearing. When mental man breathes out, he exhales thought, word or deed. And yet the being is not complete. The spiritual man must breathe too. The soul has to breathe to be spiritually alive. One must absorb and transmit the living breath and food of the soul. It must breathe in love.

The two functions of the soul are to know and to love. The practice of mediumship channels that knowledge and love - from one soul to another, and from your inner self to your outer self.

The second major function of mediumship is to bind the three

52

levels (physical, mental and spiritual) of man together. It does so by love. To see man in his natural setting as a physical, mental and spiritual being, you can appreciate the need for a binding power, a directive force. This binding and directing is the function of mediumship.

The true priest is the man who allows to flow through his veins the living breath of love. Religion need have no name, but its function has to be understood. It binds together philosophy and science, and makes more complete the picture of creation. It inspires and directs the natural flow of man's energy and talent.

How does it do this? It does it quietly and simply by providing an atmosphere of love in which man's body, mind and spirit can grow.

It encourages the physical expression of love and compassion at all levels. It reinforces a world view which supports rather than threatens man; it teaches positive, not negative thinking; it encourages competition only for the good of others, not at their expense; it nurtures tolerance and teaches that each man has (and must have) his own pathway to God and understanding. It inspires the old to say to the young: "This is what we did. Now we're going to help you do even better."

This is the attitude that a natural, living religion should engender. And mediumship in its highest and purest form is the activity it encourages.

Returning to nature for a moment, the wise farmer knows that to obtain the best results he must firstly acquire the finest possible seeds. He must provide the most suitable soil and environment.

If our seeds (our mediums) are to be selected from society, it follows that we should in every possible way do all in our power to raise the standard of the common man. It is a sheer waste of time to grow crops which no one is sufficiently evolved to use. It is equally absurd and futile to develop a standard of mediumship for which (because of the lack of education) there can be no appreciation.

Great strides have been made in education. We probably have more formal education today than ever before. The result is that our minds are alert to many things. Yet they are numbed to others. We started off by exploring the idea of materialism and how Spiritualism is (in a sense) its opposite. A materialistic education will effectively block any growth of appreciation of mediumship, because materialism will label such things as not real.

If we are looking for good mediumship, if we are looking for an appreciative audience for it, our first step is to ensure that we teach people the existence and value of the life in the body. Once this reality is established, we can go forward.

Sometimes Spiritualists can do this with individuals with the almost-shock tactics of clairvoyance when they prove that life is not determined by or restricted to a functioning physical body. It would be much easier if the spiritual side of their education was not neglected. Then they would not have to re-learn their natures.

In an environment where mediums were no longer forced to prove the existence of Spirit at every turn, they could channel guidance, reassurance, higher teaching and spiritual health, much more effectively.

Imagine a student coming to an English teacher for tutoring. The session will last for one hour. For the first half, the English teacher has to prove he is appropriately qualified. And remember this has to happen at the beginning of every session. How ridiculous! What a waste of time!

Yet when we go for a private sitting, that is exactly what occurs as the medium brings us evidence of survival. In fact, we might be upset if that were not the case. The idea is bad enough when we compare it to the case of the English teacher, but how horrifying to think of a doctor or a surgeon having to go through the same rigmarole before using their skills to help us!

Here are people ready and willing to serve. What would happen if, before every consultation, every operation, they wasted valuable time proving they were capable, or that medical science was effective. Over the years, Spiritualists have worked their way into this ridiculous situation: it is time they worked their way back out again if they want to make the most use of their mediumship. It is time they worked their way out of entertainment and into service.

One of the greatest weaknesses of Spiritualism today is that too many mediums desire the prestige of public popularity. We should instruct them that their first concern ought to be for the truth and its most effective application in life. There is no point in having the truth if you do nothing constructive with it.

But it is not only the presentation of mediumship which needs to be changed: it is its reception. I said we need a people-based religion. The large percentage, however, of those attending Spiritualist meetings are only prepared to tolerate listening to an address if there is the hope that afterwards they will be told, "All will be well." As a result, any worthwhile philosophy is replaced by nice-sounding but meaningless platitudes. Real evidence of spirit communion gives way to drivel, stuff and nonsense.

Mediumship, like life, is subject to natural laws. One can only transmit in proportion to what one is able to absorb. So the medium and the congregation need to work on improving their abilities to think, feel and care if they wish like-minded spirit people to work with and for them.

The poet may write the most exquisite lines about a rose, but a man not fond of reading will absorb those words merely as "something about a rose." Those in the spirit world can transmit only what we with all our limitations can absorb. In other words, spirit people are really as dependent upon us as we are upon them. Communication with that life has to be communion : it has to be a contract where both parties are truly bound to work very hard to extend their capacities for transmission and absorption.

If we believe that mediumship is a one-way process where the medium sits passively to receive and does nothing beforehand by way of preparation, Spirit has little chance to do anything very remarkable.

The work of the Spiritualist extends far beyond the walls of a seance room, beyond churches and psychic centres. It has to embrace every aspect of life. All nature, all life, forms the workplace of the Spiritualist. Table-rapping is almost irrelevant, and clairvoyance not the sum total of Spiritualism. There is a larger vision to behold.

Our services do not extend solely to those who attend our churches and seances; are not restricted to any particular class or group. We are the servants of all humanity, of all men, in proportion to the evolution of their soul consciousness, and subject to the higher power of love. Our service is the intervention of common sense - natural philosophy.

It is a means of knowledge taking the place of ignorance. It is the intervention of truth, the dawn of understanding, the dawn of love. This is the meaning of Divine Intervention. When we are prepared to work at it, it can work all the time.

It is often said that mediumship is not the same as it was; there is so little physical phenomena now; the great platform mediums seem to have had their day. In faint reply, others bewail the fact that we haven't the time to sit as we used to, that people cannot attend circles as regularly as in years gone by. There is a distrust of new methods and approaches.

To all this nostalgia, I would say: "Mediumship should not be the same as yesterday. Where would any other science be if it stuck to the practices of a hundred years ago? What would life be like in our present society if industry still conformed to Victorian methods of production, or if employers and governments still tried to impose the systems of living and working that pertained to the Dark Ages?"

Spiritualism is the study and rejoicing of the life in the body. Life manifests itself through change, constant change. Where there is no change, there is death, cessation of life. This simple statement applies equally to things physical, emotional, mental and spiritual. Where there is no change, there is no life.

If the quality of mediumship deteriorates, it will be because we are trying to work against natural law. If life is always changing, our understanding of it has to alter too. Because we are trying to hold on to yesterday's symbols, instead of reaching out toward today's truth, we are denying mediumship. If we want mediumship constantly to verify what we learned yesterday - that our loved ones are not dead, that we do not die, that life in the spirit world is such and such a way — we have doomed it from the start.

Doomed it? Yes. Because mediumship starts from what we know, and reaches out beyond that for what we do not know. It is progressive, not regressive. We do not need mediumship to tell us what we already know.

Go back to nature. Think of the fragrant sweet pea. It starts as nothing more than a fragile seedling. It puts out a tendril and begins its climb. One after another it reaches out to take hold of a support and latches on to it. That way the plant grows, develops, reaches for the sun and produces its wonderful perfumed flowers. Well, if we were sweet peas, our mediumship would be our tendrils which allow us to grow ever "onward and upward."

Sadly we are using tendrils to hold on to the beliefs and symbols of yesterday instead of reaching out towards the truth of today. The natural drift of life is to cast off the restrictions of conformity and to break free from the curse of smug indifference. Everything you see in life is the promise, the symbol of some greater manifestation of fuller life. Every new skill or activity we develop is a prophecy of an even higher skill or activity. The acorn is the prophecy of the oak. The stone is the promise that one day a wall shall be built, a house, then a city. It has always been like that. It always will be.

The fact is that symbols linger on far too long. It is the function of mediumship to allow new and higher knowledge, wisdom, power and love to flow through man. It is its function to uproot the dead wood of conformity and passe ideas. Its purpose is to allow the light of a new morning to flood in upon us, to allow the finest forms of human kind to evolve on earth.

We cannot attain natural mediumship unless we are prepared to pay the natural price. Nature is a just and honest master. The end product or fruit of your mediumship will be an indication of many things. It quality will tell something of the kind of person you are, what sort of atmosphere or environment you have worked in, how much effort and hard work you have put in.

The way to achieve fine mediumship is hard, but it is just. You cannot bribe nature: tears will always be the price of joy. Only the stout heart prepared to accept defeat will be able to taste real victory. Only those who are prepared to fail with courage and bravely face failure again and again can embrace the true flower of success.

If a plant is to be healthy, it has to take its natural time to grow. There is no short cut to perfection or to excellence. We progress step by step. We cannot skip one or two in the hope of achieving excellence more quickly. It is little use in trying to become angels until we learn to be men. Material values can only retain their attraction for so long.

In due time, the world will need something that is more real;

something which is more solid, something that man instinctively inside himself and will recognise. When the time is right, man will know with a sense - a sense of feeling - which will enable him to say: "This is real! I know it is. Not with a part of my being, not with emotion or intelligence, not with my prejudice, but with my self I know this to be right and just."

Every manifestation of life, every great work, whether it be a work of science, politics, philosophy, art or religion, has to be paid for in advance. All men who have become truly great, whether as a scientist, politician, philosopher, artist or priest, have known moments of sacred silence, moments when they have been moved by a strange, compelling force to withdraw from the public view.

Dedication to their high calling, constancy of purpose, a deep compassion and love for their fellow men: all these have made the moment right for the true seance to be held. In the stillness of the study, laboratory, studio or workshop, soul is touched by soul. There is no sudden burst of light, no streaming flood of power.

Slowly, painfully, each word, each movement, is born in agonising pain and torment. The aspiring mind, the bleeding heart, the long tortuous battle, continues until at last the work is done and the moment of communion is over. Then a new peace descends.

Still trembling, still perspiring, the soul gazes, scarce able to believe the beauty it now sees; scarce able to believe the profundity of this fresh revelation. Now ecstasy grips his being as quietly he re-lives each precious moment of agony, pain and torment. Silently he breathes deep into his being the memory of his suffering as though it were the sweetest breath of life for in his heart he knows that humanity as yet unborn shall be the richer because of his seance with the divine.

This is the experience of mediumship at its highest. It is mediumship reaching out to the life, knowledge and love beyond our own. It is the way we grow. It is a natural process of evolution. Once we become aware of it, it is the basis of a natural philosophy of life.

What, then, must be our verdict on natural philosophy? In the first place, it is not man-evolved : it unfolds itself as naturally as we survive in our necessary environment. Be it soon or late, the day will come when the world will see that Spiritualism can do more than any other movement to make available the necessary knowledge in providing the required environment.

Already there is evidence that the more enlightened governments and employers realise that natural philosophy pays. It is sound economics. By paying a better wage, by providing better living standards and working conditions, productivity and profits are higher than ever before when men and workers were regarded merely as slaves.

It is a verdict of Nemesis. Flick knives, gang warfare, exploitation, drug taking, class and racial hatred, and parasites of society are recognised to be the natural legacy of poverty, ignorance and war. It is a verdict which will permit no deception or lie.

In due time, the world will see us for what we are. Then the big head will not be able to hide the little mind, neither will the loud voice disguise the fact that it has nothing to say.

Let us put on our designer clothes and fine jewellery : if the strength of our character does not match, we shall be seen as naked and the poverty of our souls witnessed. It is a verdict which exposes the shallow mockery of artificial status and solemnity.

Expressions of piety adorned in gorgeous vestments and the slow tread of religious processions with their holier-than-thou attitude, the bland worship of dead creeds, out-dated symbols, cannot give us pure religion, cannot give us the true priest any more than a good media image can give us a true statesman.

Moans and groans, shivers and shakes, stuttering and spluttering, whims and fancies, cannot give us pure knowledge, cannot give us pure Spiritualism, cannot and will not give us true mediumship.

We must be realistic in our endeavour to present Spiritualism to the world. We need to feel conscious of a sense of holy dedication in our work. The moment is opportune for a measure of a portion of natural philosophy to unfold itself. Spirit intelligences are eager to assist us in this great task.

Their knowledge will spring forth and blend itself with ours...if we prove ourselves capable of receiving it. From the spiritual universe a power greater than ours awaits the signal of our souls. An order of divinity is there to enshroud us.

A flower of unutterable beauty awaits to be born and shed its precious fragrance upon our earth. Let us commit the seeing eye, the feeling heart, the living soul, to know that the temple of the universe awaits our worship. Let us know one moment of sacred stillness wherein we may be still, that our souls may hear the silent eloquence of the heavens proclaim nature's eternal message, "Be still and know that I am God." For that is the true mediumship of natural philosophy.

Chapter Seven

STRAW INTO GOLD

WHATEVER I have achieved in my life, my main effort has been to explain about the nature of Spirit, and to encourage its growth. "Describe spirit," you say.

Spirit simply is. Spirit is the state of being. In its most primitive state it has no form; it just is. But in its most primitive state it has (within this being) the potential for everything: size, mass, speed, direction, magnetism, personality. You name it, spirit could become it.

As you are reading this, you may be trying hard at understanding the text, or arguing with it, but you are not working at being. That comes naturally, without any thought or effort on your part at all. You can't stop being if you want to, although you can stop reading. You can't stop being, because you are Spirit, and Spirit is being everywhere in some form or other.

You can't stop being, but you can stop reading. You can start to sing; you can go for a walk. All the things you can do are not those you can do with Spirit; they are ones you can do with the products of spirit. Spirit has manifested itself in matter as your body, as this book, as the room you are sitting in. You have some control over its manifestations, but none over the nature of Spirit itself.

Everything is a manifestation of Spirit. This means that if you want to understand anything about Spirit, you need only look around you for the answer. If you look carefully and patiently enough, you will find the answer literally staring you in the face. Perhaps that's why artists and thinkers so often find their inspiration in nature.

Now if you ask me how Spirit manifests, I have to say I don't know. An easy answer is, "By the will of God," but that doesn't really explain much. It only gives you further questions to ask about the nature of God and will.

However, on the principle that you can tell a little about a man from the things he does, we can tell a little about Spirit from the manifestations it makes. We can tell more about it if we can identify trends, patterns or meaningful significance in the manifestations. Although we may not understand it fully, we can learn to make the best use of it within the limitations of our understanding.

Once man used water to quench his thirst, later to power the steam train, and later still to generate electricity as well. As we learn to understand Spirit more fully, we can use it more effectively and beneficially.

To understand, we look for order, we look for a pattern or natural sequence: day must follow night, and night the dying day; stars rise and set, only to rise again. Each incident of life is a natural sequence from a preceding incident. Every moment of time is the parent of the future moment. All form is the result of a cause. So, in turn, each cause is only the effect of a previous cause.

Observation of this regular pulse or rhythm in the flow of life enables us to anticipate events and manifestations. It is in this way that we are able to calculate, and to develop the ability to judge, assess and decide. As soon as we start talking about our ability to make decisions, we make the assumption that we have at least some degree of free choice. Is that really so? Have we, in fact, any real freedom of choice?

Most materialist philosophers would deny that the individual has, in the true sense, the power of personal freedom of choice. Indeed, in the final analysis, personal choice would be contrary to the belief of most religious sects. If it is true that all life is in an orderly pattern or sequence based on the law of cause and effect, it would seem that all judgement and decision is inevitable. To say of anything that it is an effect of a previous cause, is to claim that the previous cause is itself an effect of a previous cause and so on, ad infinitum.

Are we then to assume there can be no voluntary life, no vital life? Are we nothing more than mechanical robots clothed with the illusion that we have some degree of choice or freedom? Can it be that no moment of time can unfold or reveal anything more than what is already fixed and determined in the first absolute cause?

If that is the case, what point is there in planning? The outcome would seem to be inevitable. Yet we know from our common experience that if you plan something before you do it, it is more likely to be successful than if you do it any old how. Planning pays off. This has to be an indication that there is choice somewhere along the line in our lives.

Obviously, the process of cause and effect has much to teach us concerning the tendency and inclination of life, but equally it must be obvious that cause and effect is only an indication of a law, and not the law itself. To maintain that cause and effect is the absolute law of life would be to grant that all forms of life, all moments, moods and experiences are vital and necessary.

The very fact that man can even consider whether or not spiritual law is a reality indicates he is not content to regard life simply as a process of automation. We behave as if we were free. Indeed, the commonsense and higher instincts of man rebel and call out in protest against all forms of disorder and confusion. These higher instincts refuse to accept that all falsehood, evil, pain and disease are vital and necessary effects of an unalterable cause.

It may well be that much of the growth and development of human life can be explained by the laws of mathematics or the mechanical processes of the universe. And science and philosophy might well be justified in seeking their conclusions or confirmations by the use of logic and reasoning based on sequential patterns of cause and effect. But at some point, each of these methods will break down.

The nature of life has a tendency which is both voluntary and vital. It is this tendency of vital life to engage itself in an unceasing struggle, to break free from the chains of this apparently fixed and eternal order, which exposes the severe limitations of all materialistic science and philosophy. If all was cause and effect, why should man struggle to change conditions, why should he seek for improvement or growth? His whole life is lived with the intent of improving life and providing freedom to choose or design the next effect and stimulate the next cause.

Within bounds, cause and effect is a tool to be used, not a

master to be obeyed. When we look for our plan for development, we may therefore consider that we are not totally determined by cause and effect: we are merely limited by it.

And yet it is in these limitations that we find just the clues we need to establish the brighter nature of life. If I were to tell you that I have ten objects, at that moment, you would perceive that I have one object, and two and three and all the sequential units between one and ten. There can never be any alternative to this perception. Never can I have the total ten without also having the total one, two, three and so on up to ten. There is no freedom here. The reason is that we are dealing with mathematical concepts which cannot be changed.

Let us now assume I want to make an alteration. It is possible to make an addition, to multiply, to divide, to subtract, but whichever alteration I make, I seek for the answer by seeking for something that is fixed already: for the answer to every mathematical problem already exists. That answer can never be varied.

It is an answer which is entirely outside the scope of, or the influence of, man. There never was, there never can be, a moment in time which can alter the fact that one plus one equals two. We have no freedom to change principles. Our understanding of them may develop, but we cannot change them.

Herein lie the two limitations which no materialistic philosophy has been able to overcome. Mathematical and mechanical methods survive only because they are (firstly) subject to repetition and (secondly) are not subject to the influence of time.

This is the great divide. This is the gulf between matter and Spirit - the difference between appearance and reality. We have to understand this before we can go forward in the promotion of our spiritual growth. No form of animate life is ever capable of exact repetition. Life is in a constant state of becoming. This is one of the few fundamentals of which we can be absolutely sure.

How can we be sure that this is so? Because one of the things which life must have in order to be is time. In the magnificent language of Plato, "God, unable to make the world eternal, gave it time: a moving image of eternity."

Time is the measure of change. It is our perception of change. Time is the ever-flowing point which moves on, gnaws its unrelenting teeth into all that is. No form of life can for a single instant be free of its mark. There was no womb from which it sprang. There is no grave which can imprison it.

Time is not just eternal or to be used in the abstract sense: it is a positive force before whose august glory even the Gods must bow. Not only is time in a constant state of flow, it is in a constant state of change. Moment follows moment. And each moment is different.

This explains why so many experiments in the realms of the psychic seem to fall down or prove inconclusive. The psychic is animate — alive. It changes all the time and cannot exactly repeat a previous manifestation as a mechanical experiment might do.

There are experiences in life which give us so much pleasure that we desire to repeat them, but it is only in the symbolic, mathematical or mechanical sense that anything can really be repeated. Experiences may seem to be the same, but can never be an exact repetition.

Often our perception will not be as sharp or keen enough to discern the difference, but nevertheless it is there. Such is the gradual, noiseless stealth by which time moves, that seldom can we pinpoint any actual moment of change. For social and legal purposes, we name actual moments in which we say a person becomes an adult or enters old age, but we all know that moments so named are symbolic rather than actual.

Time is. But if time is to have a meaning, there must be something to exist in time. This something we call spiritual force or vital force. I shall refer to it as "Spirit." Spirit, in order for us to be aware of it, must have some matter on which it can work or through which it can breathe or express itself. The potter requires clay through which to express himself; the musician, a musical instrument. I need words to express myself, and paper and print to express myself to you.

It holds then, as I said before, that all matter has something to say concerning the nature of Spirit. The more animate or alive matter is, the closer and more successful its contact with Spirit. Matter exists. It exists because Spirit expresses itself. Spirit has need of matter because matter is the body of Spirit. Through this body Spirit strives to breathe, struggles to express itself.

All the countless species are indications of the efforts of Spirit to pour itself through matter. The story of the encounter of Spirit with matter is surely one of the very best use of resources, for using Spirit plus matter plus environment, all the many realms and forms of life have emerged. Every moment of every day, the vast variety of vegetation and animal life continues to multiply.

Think of the building that goes on every day, day after day. Think of the ceaseless flow of nature's manufacture. The concept that all this endless variety has emerged and continues to emerge from the original potential of Spirit may be difficult to accept. Yet it is nevertheless true that there is no more and no less space, matter and energy now than there was two hundred thousand years ago.

You cannot glance over the story of evolution without being drawn to the conclusion that there is involved here something more than matter and environment. Between all kingdoms and realms and orders of life (when they are functioning properly) there is harmony. There are always complementary relationships which are suggestive of purpose and a sense of direction. It is as though both the earth and the worm say to each other, "I am in order that you might be."

All vegetation takes up the theme. So too does the animal and human kingdom. Further, above and beyond all material, physical manifestation and expression, we hear the all-embracing voice of solar energy exclaiming: "You are, but only because I am. And I am because you are."

But it is not in solar energy or environment, not in the kingdom of material or physical life, that we shall find the answer we seek. All the various species of life are indications of the vital efforts of Spirit to breathe through environment and matter more and even more of its creative living force. All life as we know it is the result of Spirit's desire to obtain greater and fuller expression of freedom. Spirit is a constant, eternal, yearning to be. To be itself, to be the poet of all poetry, the artist of all art, the music of all symphony, harmony and melody. To be the creator of creation.

In trying to seek the direction of life, we are obliged to look along an endless path. There is no final goal, no absolute end product. The direction of Spirit and life is onward; the tendency of life and Spirit is to become. This does not mean that all species or forms of life were intended or meant to be. Many — and indeed tremendous — are the obstacles which Spirit has had to encounter in its struggle for expression. Obstacles which seem overwhelmingly powerful in their magnitude are forever and ever appearing. They make their repeated attempt to ravage and destroy the whole pattern of life's evolving theme. And yet all efforts to smash or shatter the poise of nature have so far failed.

These, the indwelling will of life forces, remain still unmoved. It would appear that this indwelling spark of life is possessed of the ability to correct its own errors. And thus the moments of pain which swell into mighty crescendoes of tortuous, tormenting affliction, are transformed into the living, breathing breath of life. The tendency of life remains in its eternal state of becoming. Its direction is ever on.

I wonder if you remember the story of Rumplestiltskin? A fairy story, of course, but it has more than just an entertainment value. Let me refresh your memory.

A peasant and his daughter were extremely poor. Although she was a beautiful young maiden, there seemed little chance of any joy in life as they could only just scrape a living. The girl supplemented the little her father made by spinning, but one evening - working hard as she had done all day — she realised they could not make ends meet, and started to cry.

Her weeping stopped when she espied a strange little man dancing in front of her to attract her attention. He promised to spin straw into gold for her. Although the maiden did not believe him, she brought a bale of straw to him. He commanded that she leave him in peace, which she did. All through the night she could hear the whirring of the spinning wheel. And in the morning when the strange little man had disappeared, she found the straw had indeed been spun into pure gold.

Her father was enchanted, kept some of the gold and used the rest to provide a dowry for his daughter to marry a rich farmer or king (depending on the version you read).

Now, figuratively speaking, it is the function of the wise man to spin gold out of straw. Straw is the apparently useless remains of life. We can see it as memories, impressions, suffering, etc. They all seem of no practical use. But the knowing little man spins gold out of this: the gold of wisdom or understanding in our terms. He teaches us that with skill and effort we can make significance from what was insignificant.

What effect can this have on our lives? Put at its most basic, it allows us to be creative: the maiden became a wife and mother (as well as a nice little earner!). All this because she made use of this wisdom. He had the knowledge, she had the love. By himself, the strange little man could do nothing. On her own, the maiden was driven almost to despair. Working together, they allowed the creative expression of life to happen.

Significantly, however, she could only continue in her nurturing role as mother by struggling to know by herself. She finally achieves this symbolically by learning his name. The maiden and the wise little man no longer exist: she marries and he disappears. In effect the two have been integrated into one, and thus the wise wife (love and wisdom together) ends the story, entitled to the joy and creativity she has.

Fairy tale or fable, we can learn from many a source. From the valueless: ourselves, our lives, perhaps the original space itself: we weave all the gold of creation.

One of the difficult problems which philosophy has to solve is the existence of species or forms which are not necessary to the development of further spiritual life. If, as most philosophers agree, life proceeds because of its pleasure instinct, why does there persist in life so much that is unpleasant? Our fairy tale helps us to come to terms with this.

The most common error philosophy makes is to assume that all forms of life which exist were deliberate calculations and intentions. But as I have already explained, life more than anything else, is a tendency to act on inert matter, to enliven it. The direction of this action is not predetermined. Hence the unforseeable variety of forms which life, in evolving, sows along its path.

Creation, as we know it, is the result not so much of an orderly sequence of development, but from sudden, impulsive bursts of inspired spontaneity. That there is a degree of order and sequential development, we, of course, accept, but life refuses to be tied down to one set pattern. On the surface it may appear that evolution proceeds in a calm, orderly, intelligent fashion. But the indwelling life force is never satisfied.

Underneath the intelligent form, the orderly rhythm or conscious effort, is the instinctive psychic force of unconscious life. It is the unconscious or psychic force which unceasingly is in this state of becoming. This means that from every moment in time, from every sensation, emotion and experience, psychic life is all the while adding to itself new force and energy.

This building up process continues until there is such a degree of force that its intensity of desire explodes. The explosion will achieve something of its aim, but as an end result of the explosive outburst, while the target is reached, the force of the vital impetus is such that many smaller fragments will flee from the main force and fly forth into all kinds of unforseeable directions.

It is in the human kingdom that we are committed to witness the meeting point of so many of life's forces. Here surely we have arrived at one of the high level marks of creative life. Through mankind, nature speaks with an eloquence not possible in any other kingdom, world or sphere.

In man, vital life becomes both poem and poet, art and artist, invention and inventor, slave and master, lord and servant. All these things become one in man. Reality melts into dream and dream steps forth into the new day, declaring itself real.

Reality and dream : which is which? Hindu teaching explains that all we consider real, all that our senses tell us about, is maya or illusion. Only the formless is real, it says. Of course, that is confusing to us, and not much use in our workaday lives. However, whatever you choose to believe as being real, man is the transformer of it.

Think about it. No tool that we use, no piece of furniture in our homes, nothing that has ever been produced was not a thought first. Someone had the idea and then made the object. All our man-made physical reality has its source in the mind (in a dream if you like).

Man made that dream into a reality. Virtually all our actions stem from our "intangible" consciousness. How we feel about our life today, or Chopin, or an incident at work, is as a result of some goings-on in our heads. One action may be considered good today, yet exactly the same action tomorrow may fill us with outrage. The physical condition may not change, but the attitude (the non-physical attitude) has. What goes on in man's head determines his reality. His dreams make reality. And reality makes his dream for we are often stimulated into thought by some physical incident or other. We are the spinners of straw into gold.

We are interested in encouraging spiritual development in man. Ironically, man is the tool by which Spirit develops, in a sense. If Spirit can express itself through all forms of energy, the mental energy - the energy of consciousness in man - is probably the highest form that we have yet recognised. Spirit expresses itself in energy.

That energy in turn expresses itself in matter - atomic structures if you like. When such structures are imbued with more energy, they become animate and can further develop their own structures (as plants do). Although not consciously, they can create replicas of themselves as animals do. But in man's consciousness, in his developed mind, as Spirit infuses his being more and more, he becomes his own creator, a god in the making.

If in man nature has touched a new height, it has also reached a new depth. Because of the greater sense of choice, the greater freedom to make decisions that vital life finds in man, there is an increase in the possible dangers of expression through him. There are also many more unnecessary, foolish and downright wrong decisions.

Up until this point of developing mind, there has been little need for morality. Life proceeded in a natural and instinctive way and exhibited a psychic order. The only moral standard was to seek for the greatest possible protection and the greatest possible gain. The policy of nature is based upon one maxim: survival of the fittest.

Its only science is to dissolve or to be dissolved, absorb or be absorbed. The religion of early life had but one creed : to be. There was only one prayer - to be freed from the degree of restriction of their given kingdom. Life in the lower kingdom to a large extent seems to be self organised.

This is not so in the human kingdom where, because of a new-found mobility and greater versatility, the dwelling of a fuller awareness and intelligent perception, the exceedingly complex

70

nature of man himself has reached beyond the restrictions of the animal kingdom. His is the dawning of a fuller awareness and intelligent perception. His nature has become exceedingly complex because he has so many feelings, talents, passions, emotions and impulses, each holding its sway over the decisions he makes. In fact, he has become a world in miniature within himself.

A new form of deliberate and calculated organisation became an urgent need and a grim necessity for him. Human power, talents and virtues had to be marshalled. A plan had to be shaped which would concern itself with the architecture of social order and human behaviour. Conflicting desires, emotions and passions had to be unravelled and disentangled.

Man has had to ask, "How can the freedom I need be made to function within the restriction of life?" Religion, politics, science and philosophy have all in their turn tried to answer this question.

Knowledge, we are told, is power. But just as wood does not become a fuel until it is placed on the fire, so knowledge does not become power until it is on fire. Education itself is not enough. Knowledge is not enough.

To become power, knowledge must become alight and burn its way through the walls and barriers of wrong ideas and the evils of ignorance and superstition.

One of the vital functions of Spiritualism is to make available to men the knowledge of spiritual life. Such knowledge, if rightly used, could give birth to a higher morality. Politics, science, religion and philosophy, purified and enriched by this knowledge could pour new benefits into every direction of human life.

Chapter Eight

MAKING SPIRITUALISM WORK BETTER

THE introduction of new knowledge was the motivation behind the early, enlightened Spiritualists. When the pioneers of modern Spiritualism were filling halls over a century ago, they were claiming that their philosophy would revolutionise the world, but few people today would agree that it has done so. So why doesn't it work?

Truly, it would not be correct to say it doesn't work. What I would say is that it doesn't work as well as it might. It does not have the universal effect that it should.

There are several reasons why it is not working as well as it might. Let's start with this one: you can't make something work — and you certainly can't make it work well—if you are not aware of its existence. That is the situation that many people are in.

Because their education ignores the spiritual dimension, they don't think about Spirit, don't think Spirit exists, don't think Spirit can be significant. It is relegated to the fringes of life.

If Spiritualists wish to be significantly useful to their fellows, firstly they must concentrate on effective methods of education. Not propagation, not dogmatising, but the drawing out of interested students an understanding of the reality of Spirit.

Here is another reason for Spiritualism's unimpressive track record: people see so-called Spiritualists and are put off. I wish I could write this flippantly, but I cannot. The greatest threat to Spiritualism comes from Spiritualists: Spiritualists who are trying to organise what has not yet evolved; to demonstrate mediumship which has not yet been developed.

It is also sadly true that too many Spiritualists are more

concerned with their personal prestige than with the prestige of Spiritualism. This undermines its philosophy and its credibility. For some enthusiastic Spiritualists, to hold high office is considered more important than being effective as a medium. The seance room is being sacrificed upon the altars of administration and committees.

Psychic and spiritual vision is being dimmed by the fogs created by our own self-conceit, and dreams of being a "famous medium." It seems too we have yet to learn that cheap, childish outrage against other Spiritualists who dare to think differently from us, is not only a useless waste of energy, but thwarts and hinders the natural flow of true natural spiritual power.

Unless Spiritualists are rich in understanding, unless they are wellsprings of love, unless they can demonstrate their effectiveness in life, why should anyone want to take an interest in their philosophy?

Coupled to these two is a third reason. People of all denominations, ages and abilities may be aware of the power of Spirit (or the spiritual), but do not know (or perhaps have just forgotten) how it works. That's the same as saying that ancient peoples knew of the existence of electricity, but not knowing how it worked, they could not harness its power. They could not put it to good and effective use.

The religious-minded of many denominations, as well as Spiritualism, are not putting the spiritual to its best and most effective use.

It's difficult to know what to do about a situation like this, especially in a time like ours when whole societies are overthrowing their traditional ideologies and striving towards a better, finer life. Democracy alone is not the answer to a hungry, ex-totalitarian state. Enterprise cannot engender true progress while success is measured exclusively in financial or material terms. Quality of life is what people are seeking, even although they may have only the vaguest notion of what quality comprises.

It is my concern that people be taught that one of life's components is spiritual. Unless this element in man is recognised and satisfied, his other achievements will leave him always with a tinge of disappointment. I am not asking that people look again to religious doctrine or find a new faith. If that's what they need, they will search for that too. I am asking that they be made aware of their higher potential, that they are offered the opportunity to attain it. A simple approach to such attainment is as follows:

1. Acquire knowledge of spiritual development.

2. Make every effort and sacrifice to develop the highest and finest standards of spiritual awareness or mediumship.

3. Use whatever knowledge or power is achieved thereby for the benefit and enrichment of the entire human family.

Step one: what have we learned about spiritual development?

We have learned that it is the beginning stuff of the universe; that in space, spirit has the potential to do and be everything.

Spirit expresses itself through energy and matter.

We may learn about it through observing our own bodies and our entire environment, because all physical things are expressions of spirit.

We have learned that it is not restricted to the rigid laws of cause and effect as mechanical or mathematical things are.

It operates freely and spontaneously within the larger restriction of principles.

When matter, Spirit and environment are in harmony, Spirit will produce a further variety of expression.

As Spirit breaks free into a new expression, some of its creative energy will spin off and may evolve a further, unexpected variety.

We have learned that Spirit changes; that it is constantly becoming.

Because it changes, it experiences time, as time is simply the perception of changes.

We have learned that it cannot repeat anything exactly, and that man acts as a transformer of the subtler energy of Spirit into the denser material of his own creations

We might even suggest from this that the consciousness of God is the transformer through which all forms manifest.

Only as we understand the nature of this Spirit can we begin to plan how best to develop it.

Right, then, you have put yourself in the position of trainer/ teacher/developer. Because you want to be of service to mankind, and make a meaningful life for yourself, where do you go from here? How are you going to develop the spiritual natures of others?

First of all, you don't start with the others. You begin with yourself. And in doing so, don't be surprised if the only student you ever have is yourself. Certainly, I wouldn't bother yourself looking for students. If you have something worthwhile to offer, they will come to you without you asking. If they think you have nothing to offer, they will leave you in peace, rightly or wrongly. It is best for all concerned if you just count the blessing of such peace and privacy, and get on with the student who is you.

How do you start your training? You meditate. You practise stillness and silence until you are comfortable with yourself and can rest content in your own company. Then you continue to meditate for the rest of your life.

I say this because, in a sense, meditation is spiritual breathing and without its constant practise you will allow the continual distractions of the physical world to persuade you that they are more important than the task you have set yourself.

If you never get beyond this stage in your "training," you will have gone a long way. Do not fret about it.

If you wish to continue, you may invite your conscious mind (or your intellect) to become involved.

Use your mind to remind yourself that Spirit has the potential to do and be everything. Don't confuse Spirit here with spirit people. We are talking here of the life force of the universe. The stuff that you are made of.

Remind yourself that with preparation and hard work, aspiration and prayer, you and the world have the potential to do all things. In other words, don't limit you own personal spirit by constantly saying "I can't." If you need to, if it is good, if you have striven towards your goal, you — perhaps with the help of others — probably can. Even if your goal is unattainable, you will learn why eventually and grow wiser as a result. In the meanwhile, ask yourself if "I can't" really means, "I won't."

Continue to think of Spirit in your meditation, and work on the idea that it is the beginning stuff of the universe.

If that is the case, then think of your relationship with all other things: people, places, animals, ideas, everything. They are all connected. You are all part of each other. Take as many years as you like to meditate on that. You will grow in your understanding of it. As you do so, put your understanding into action. This is not a plea to be trendy and environmental. It is a plea to be meaningfully, lovingly and respectfully part of the environment. Live out your understanding in practical terms.

Remember that you are free and spontaneous. You are not a set of mathematical calculations: you are never entirely predictable. This will give you a sense of freedom which is, in fact, the breath of life. You are not a robot. If anything, you are more like the passenger in the car. You are in charge of where you want to go. As you grow older, the car may not serve you quite as well, but it can never dictate to you entirely. You can always get out and walk when things get difficult!

Value spontaneity, and know that you can never repeat any thing exactly. Each time life is a little different. For that reason (if you allow it to be) it is always interesting. For Spirit to grow, it has to have free expression, and needs an interested audience. Be spontaneous, be interested. That way you have provided a good environment for growth.

Learn the value of harmony. It is like sunshine to plants: without it there is no growth. Harmony is the result of love. It is a loving approach, a loving interpretation, a loving coming-together. Practise harmony in music, in colour, form, dance, in ideas, in friendship, in nature, in silence.

Dare to enjoy change and the unexpected. If you channel your efforts to develop a spiritual gift, you may be disappointed if you do not attain it. But you might also be greatly surprised that a completely different sensitivity or ability arises in you. Of course, you should strive for a goal, but there is never any need to be blinkered in your approach to it. The spin-offs of spiritual development may well become a new and challenging pathway for you to follow. Explore it gladly.

Remind yourself that change is life. That way you will train yourself out of the belief that growing old is growing more dead each day. What nonsense! All change is growth; all change is experience to be learned from and developed. You are becoming more you all the time: more knowing, more loving, more spiritual

76

all the time...if you allow yourself to.

You are a spinner of straw into gold. Work on the idea that right now you are in the place which is best for you. Whatever the joys or difficulties of now, they are gift-bearing moments for you. Ask yourself what it is they bring to you, and learn from that. Every beauty is there for you to enjoy; every problem is a challenge for you to meet, beautifully. There is no moment which has no gift for you, no straw that will not become gold for you.

Each of these is an exercise in spiritual development. Each and all may take a moment and a life time. None is ever complete because life itself is never complete.

Now we have taken what we have learned about spiritual development, and tried to put it into practice. Our next instruction was to develop mediumship to the highest degree.

In fact, by practising the above simple exercises, you are developing mediumship of the most essential type because you have become the medium through which Spirit can express itself in the higher forms of loving and knowing. Everyone is, to some extent, a medium of this kind. Everyone who works at it will have some wisdom to impart to his fellow man.

You may expect me to write more specifically about circle mediumship and Spiritualist mediumship, and I shall, but the most important point must surely be that all men are mediums of Spirit.

The word "medium" is more commonly understood as the medium of spirit people. Such mediumship is more obvious than the subtle spiritual mediumship we have been considering, but it is a priceless gift, and rarer amongst men than the first. It is more specific.

Now, just as the player of a French Horn might first learn the elements of music on a penny whistle so the Spiritualist medium will learn the elements of attunement to Spirit from the same exercises that we outlined earlier. It is true that many mediums do not consciously undertake this preparation: instead they concentrate on sitting in silence in circle, practising psychometry, telepathy, visualisation, tuning in to other people, and so on.

Such practices will encourage the growth of the psychic ability and heighten and refine sensitivity to spirit people. But if Spiritualist mediumship is to be a religious activity and a service, then the medium himself must develop his own spirit in order that his mediumship (expressed as clairvoyance, direct voice, etc.) may be spiritual as well as evidential in nature. Only when the two forms of mediumship are drawn together in this way is mediumship of the highest order achieved. This is what we must aim for.

Development of such mediumship is not achieved quickly, and therefore must be approached with patience. Once it is attained, messages are not only evidential, but are uplifting and revivifying; they are constructive, giving purpose and direction to the wavering soul. Philosophy and inspiration received through such a vehicle will encourage us to reach out beyond our present limitations and to grow significantly in love and understanding.

Through this higher mediumship, the in-dwelling life force enters more freely into its own. Men with seeing eyes and feeling hearts, with breathing, knowing, living souls, become part of the ever-winding, eternally flowing dream of divine will. Through this divine will, Spirit, with inspired spontaneity, seeks ever to be, to work without ceasing, refusing to falter or abate; to labour, endure and wait until all that it foresees it will find, and what it cannot find, create.

We can become part of divine will only by giving ourselves to it. The price demanded of spiritual development is yourself. This is the law of ever-evolving life. It is this law which gives to time the nature of eternity, and infinity to space. The lower must give way to the greater, the coarse be sacrificed to culture. Every step of progress is sacrifice.

We gain by losing, grow by dividing, live by dying. This is spiritual development, spiritual progress and our very selves are the product of it.

Chapter Nine

INTO TRAINING

SINCE my time with the Lyceum, I have always run a development class, and think it is important to do so. It is a joy when you find one of your sitters developing skills with which they can serve their fellow human beings. Even when there are problems, there is always something to learn or to develop from. Teaching a class is always unpredictable and therefore enjoyable.

There are no set rules for training people in spiritual and psychic development. The trainer must just be instinctive in his approach, relying on his own sensitivity and inspiration. After all, that is what Spiritualism is all about. Of course, there has to be common sense too.

A student may find it hard to speak in public or to be sensitive to Spirit. They need encouragement to build up their confidence until they know they have the ability. In matters of presentation, they must always remember it is not the sympathy of the audience they want, but their respect: this has to be earned.

The first step is providing a confident manner of presentation. Mind you, in saying that, confidence has never stopped me from being nervous before every service I take, and I've been taking them for more than sixty years now. Nervousness is perfectly acceptable. Indeed, it is essential if you are to work at your best - just as long as the audience have no indication of it!

A good teacher can make the world of a difference to your development. I've been asked if sitters in a circle are likely to develop the same style of mediumship as their leader. This need not be the case. By all means pay attention to someone who is good, and watch how they work because that is a good way to learn.

Imitation can be good in that sense, but being yourself, expressing yourself, is always better because it is natural and true - and it is you. You are an individual in your own right. Remember that.

I first learned that lesson from my music teacher, Mr Davis. I was learning to play the cornet at the time, listening to the way he played a particular phrase of music. He didn't play it exactly as it was written, but I enjoyed the resonance he drew from the note, and spent some time practising to achieve the same effect.

When next I had a lesson with him, Mr Davis listened carefully to my performance, and smiled. He had recognised the compliment I paid him in trying to play exactly like him, but stressed in a way I have never forgotten, the importance of expressing myself as truly as I could.

Therein lies the joy and variety of individuality. Spiritual truth is not restricted to spiritual teachers.

It has been my experience that you cannot — and should not — judge a demonstration of clairvoyance by the number of times the audience says "Yes."

Lecturing one night at Bridgend, medium Walter Brooks concluded with his demonstration. He gave only one message in huge detail. It lasted twenty minutes, and each answer he received was "No." Nothing could seem worse than that. But the following week, when I was working there, the people told me that on going home, the embarrassed recipient found from the rest of his family that what Walter had said was correct.

Sometimes a "No" turns out right...in time. Moreover, a message you cannot accept at the time but find out later is correct, is a more evidential one. I say this because the recipient cannot dismiss it as the medium "reading my mind."

The medium, if he is honest with himself, knows if his message is correct by a kind of gut feeling he has. We all have this feeling, but need to be trained to become aware of it again. Some people may never claim to be mediums or clairvoyants, yet because they are sensitive to themselves, can allow their intuition to work effectively for them. My mother was not a medium, but she had a talent of reading the character of people virtually on sight. That is the same kind of gut reaction that a medium has: it simply requires natural sensitivity.

Sometimes that sensitivity works so freely that you do not notice it: it is just like second nature. My wife, Kate, lost her first husband early in the war, and returned to Troedyrhiw with her family.

For a while, they lived with relations, but the situation was proving impossible. One evening at church, she was talking over the situation with some friends. Without thinking, I interrupted with: "There's no need to worry. You shall have a house by the end of the week." It was easy to laugh at such a statement as wishful thinking, but at three o'clock that Friday afternoon, Kate answered the door to find a local landlord there with the offer of 19, Park Place. It was to be her home until she passed to Spirit.

This is just another example of how, once trained, you become aware more easily of inspiration.

Chapter Ten

UNDERSTANDING THE INFINITE

THINK of the seed reacting to the soil, air and sun. That is a form of life deriving its life as a result of association with other forms of life. If we accept that one form gains life when it reacts with a different form, we must not be afraid to consider that our form also gains life as it reacts with a different form. Once expressed, this idea seems almost too obviously true.

Couple it with a reminder that our senses limit our perception of the world so we can come to terms with it, and we must admit there is a reality beyond those senses and what they perceive.

In time, man will use not only these five physical senses, but also the senses of understanding and intuition. He will see with his body, mind and soul: see with his soul as he does in music, poetry and in all the great arts.

Man will develop a degree of sensitivity which will make him receptive to sounds unheard. He will have a mind ever ready to heal. He will feel and see with all spiritual senses. His sensitivity will render him every ready to heal and to teach in love and with knowledge. This new perception brings a new understanding.

Look at the way we understand: we realise we learn though science and philosophy, religion and art. How can these disciplines help using our understanding of the infinite?

Enlisting the aid of science will only take us so far. It will grant us the laws of nature and of sequence, but then it calmly announce, "So far and no further!" It balks at the attempt because the subject area of science is matter, and the scientific approach employs the physical senses as its most important tools.

How can the material scientist apply his skills to the non-material? How can he measure and verify when his senses (and their mechanical extensions) register nothing at all? Science then can only take us the first part of the way. If we want to explore the nature of the non-material or extra-material world, we must turn next to philosophy.

Philosophy not only produces but also examines the nature of ideas. As science uses the senses for verification, philosophy uses the mind. If a proposed solution or thesis is reasonable, then it will be acceptable to philosophy.

There are two kinds of philosophical approach: the empirical and the a priori. The empirical approach is the sister and help mate of science because it begins with physical reality and moves off from there to form conclusions based upon that reality. That is what we did when we took the suggestion that we, like seeds, react with a different form of life in order to grow.

We started with the reality of the way physical seeds react to their physical environment. This reaction is verifiable by scientific means. We then use this knowledge derived from physical reality and do so metaphorically to describe a possible non-physical reaction.

If we can detect physical signs of spiritual development, we can still check this thesis by looking at the physical behaviour of human beings. We are extrapolating physical experience into the realms of the non-physical. This physical experience is the jumping-off point of our idea.

Our flight is sustained in philosophy through the a priori approach, which takes us from the empirical knowledge to something very close to intuitive knowledge. It permits an imaginative leap to be made. It allows intuition to take over so that we can say of something, "I know that is right, even although I have no empirical evidence for it." We may be talking of the afterlife, the existence of God, or that a friend is about to phone out of the blue.

Artists have employed and expressed this kind of knowing through almost every medium you can think of: paint, music, sculpture, dance, poetry, and so on. It is here, through intuition, that man begins to move from the finite to the infinite. Intuition is defined as the immediate apprehension by the mind without

83

reasoning. Where does this knowledge come from? It has no roots in the perception of the senses. It leaves no line of logic to trace it back to its source.

If it does not come from man's physical apparatus and physical environment, we may well come to the conclusion that it arises from the mind's reaction to a higher life form. It might be a reaction to his own higher self, or another's, or even the Life Force naked of form. The intuition or inspiration of true art lifts us beyond what we know and hints at a further reality. We can guess at this further reality because the art makes us feel and perceive more intensely than ever we have done before. It makes us, for a moment, more intensely alive than we have ever been before.

When such inspiration moves a man so intensely that he finds it beyond his powers of expression, we call the experience a mystical one.

Such occurrences, although not common, have been the experiences of uncommon men throughout the ages. In its fullest intensity it is the ecstasy of the mystic; lesser and more fleeting still, it is the hunch, notion, belief of the growing sensitive. In his approach to the infinite, man passes now from the realms of philosophy through art to religion.

Although religion may not induce ecstasy, it will come nearer to explaining it than science and philosophy can. And when the fever of bliss passes, the flow ebbs away and all dies down, it is the religion which proclaims that the dream is not all over, and that the soul will not entirely resume its previous coldness.

Our religion of Spiritualism takes the religious experience, the religious reaction of man to the infinite, and tends and nourishes that experience of the infinite, to encourage its growth and development. The Spiritualist has refused to limit himself and his knowledge to the bounds of science of philosophy. He dares to share the view of the mystic that knowledge and the experience of it is limitless - infinite.

"Why am I? What am I?" These are questions man is continually posing, continually answering to the extent of his ever-growing vision. Once he stated : "Matter exists. I can see it. My senses tell me so." Then he looked beyond the matter he could see with his eyes and said: "The universe and the atom exists. I know.

My reasoning tells me so."

Shall he not then look beyond his reasoning and say, "Force, love truth, is. I know it. My soul tells me so." When he is confident in the knowing of his soul, shall he not go further and say: "Force, love, truth, is. I am force, love, truth."

The greatest part of anyone is that which life keeps veiled and obscured. This mystery within grows and unfolds according to the invisible law of its being. It is greater than force; it applies and directs force.

This directing force in man — the mystery within — is God of the infinite. It remains veiled and obscured until such times as man frees it from the shackles of his physical senses and rational thinking.

Such senses, such thinking, are, after all, only the tools used by the beginner to come to terms with the overwhelming infinity which is life. As potential master mariners upon this sea of life, we must be prepared first to do the humble work of the deckhand. Just as it would be madness to claim mastery of navigation once we can handle a scrubbing brush, so we must be prepared to use all the tools of nature, using and discarding them according to her pattern and time, for it is she who will train us towards mastery.

In such a fashion we shall, so to speak, work our way steadily up through the ranks, developing ever finer skills as we go.

So we must be true to the law of our being, the law of growth and development. When man grew to be an individual firstly through his senses, secondly through his thinking, he did not remain isolated or unconnected in his individuality. We saw that with physical maturity he bred and cared for his children. With intellectual maturity he produced new ideas and taught them to society. With each achievement, he finds he must serve.

With his spiritual maturity, he will learn to be. What will be the achievement of this being? What service does this bring? When man experiences the infinite, how can he use the fruits of his experience? He can begin to teach being to those who wish to know. Not solely through scientific fact and philosophical conjecture will he teach. He will work through spiritual unfoldment.

No one teaches a flower how to grow, but it will grow best and most strongly in conditions conducive to growth, right atmosphere, temperature, soil and so on. The man who has experienced the Infinite can encourage the growth of others in the seance room, in its sacred atmosphere and stillness. Here the aspirant will learn initially that death is a myth, not a reality.

As psychic potential becomes psychic skill, he will learn extra-sensory perception until his soul begins to react to the higher life, the extra-material life. Then as the sun's warmth stirs the seed into growth, so the life force will engender spiritual growth in man. Ultimately finite man evolves into communion with the life force. The seance room may begin as his spiritual kindergarten, but as man evolves, it becomes his university. Within its sacred silence are found all his answers, all his questions.

Statesman and scholars, healers, parents and indeed every questioning child of the universe, should be nourished here, should learn to touch the infinite here.

To a large extent, that is the seance room of tomorrow. It is so because we have allowed ignorance and sloth to inhibit the flow of life, the law of growth and development. We have accepted alike both good and indifferent evidence of the afterlife, asking only for repetition of the same rather than further stimulation towards progress.

Sometimes we have allowed spirit communion to degenerate to the level of a side show. Few of us have dared to experience the infinite. Fewer still have dared to nurture that experience in others.

Now we must dare. Dare with me. Reach out to the Infinite with me. Let each of us pray, "Let me become beautiful within." For as our beauty grows, so at last "I and the Father" become one, and man is infinite.

Chapter Eleven

VISION

"DREAMING is an act of pure imagination, attesting in all men a creative power, which, if it were available in waking, would make every man a Dante or a Shakespeare" (Hedge). "Nothing so much convinces me of the human mind as its operations in dreaming" (Clulow).

By natural tendency, all men are dreamers. The laws of evolution demand it. Life flows to us through our dreams. Whether we are asleep or awake, a great amount of our time is used up with dreaming. Why? Because the dream is the interlude or bridge which enables man to emerge from the cold, dark, night of oblivion (of not-understanding), and enter into the full warmth and freshness of full life and vision.

In fact, men are so caught up in the events of their dreams they hardly know where the dream ends and real life begins. What goes on inside his head is of more significance to each individual than the teeming life around him. Man the dreamer burns up his power, skill and talent in fighting the shadows and shams, phantoms and bubbles, of his make-believe world. He struggles to the point of exhaustion in a vain endeavour to stay the fictitious evils of his dreams. Such is the power of vision.

When we open our eyes, we take for granted our ability to see, assuming sight to be the faculty of the physical eye. But the optics of our faculty of seeing is not of itself vision. Seeing is the result of one of the most complex and sensitive of creative processes. Yes, of course the eye is essential for sight. It is through the organ of the eye, so sensitive to light, that impulses (or messages if you like) are sent to the brain with information about the state of the outside observed world.

But the transfer of information is not sight. The interpretation of the information is the sight with which we are familiar. This becomes clear when we see something the like of which we have never encountered before. We shall have trouble in seeing such a thing. In fact, we may not see it all because we have no means of interpreting the information we receive. We might disregard it entirely.

There is a story that when Captain Cook arrived in New Zealand with his sailing ships, native accounts of the visitors described the ships in detail, but made no mention of the sails. The natives did not see the sails because they had no experience of the concept of sail, never mind its reality. Instead they were amazed at the "mysteriously powered" vessels.

What we see, indeed what we can see, is determined by what we think. This means that seeing is not automatic or mechanical: it is literally a creative process. Such a sensitive and creative process is complementary to the vision of dreaming, and to the more advanced vision of wisdom. What do I mean by that?

Imagine for a moment that a life time is a training course. Hopefully, when you get to the end of the course you will have gained a qualification. The qualification is in understanding. You start at the beginning of the course with nothing. As a new-born child you have no perception and no understanding.

However, each day is full of experiences generated by the outside physical world. Each of these exercises is designed firstly to develop tools for understanding, and secondly to develop skills in the use of these tools in the same way that an apprentice has to become familiar with his tools before he can proceed to using them.

When first he uses them, he is clumsy and conscious of every move. Later, as he becomes more adept, their use becomes second nature. When finally he masters them, he is a craftsman. When his use has become so skilful that his artefacts have a value beyond the practical and utilitarian, the master becomes an artist, perhaps even a genius.

In our lives, we have first to learn to see — to use our eyes to perceive physical objects. Later we advance to more subtle seeing, looking at details of expression and gesture, for example. We are mastering our tool.

Drawing and painting encourage us to reproduce what we see. It is interesting to watch children's drawing develop in detail as their perception becomes clearer and more precise. They are practising interpreting what they see, thinking about what they see. And with experience, they learn to see more clearly.

In a way, this artistic reproduction of what they see is an externalisation of their eidetic imagery; their ability to produce mental images, to dream. So man uses his tool of sight first to create pictures stimulated by the external world, and then to produce images mentally, within his own mind. He learns to dream.

When an apprentice joiner first learns to plane wood or make joints, he may well ask, "What's the point of this?" Only once he learns how to incorporate his skills into a project which produces something useful or functional, will he be satisfied.

So with our apprentice thinker. He too may question the use of his skill of dreaming. Well, the answer is that without dreaming, he cannot maintain good mental health. Just as the health of the physical depends upon the quality and purity of its air, food and drink, so does the health of emotional, mental and spiritual man depend upon the purity and quality of his dreams.

Religion, philosophy and science each in turn has played its part in trying to rid our dreams of all unfounded fears, superstitions, emotional imbalance, personal bias and prejudice. Until this is achieved, we cannot have even a glimpse of reality.

Without dreaming, man cannot be creative. In dreaming through sleep, he reviews the experience of the day, and with further training will benefit from that experience. In dreaming in both the sleeping and waking states he can visualise, plan and create, rubbing the slate of his mind clean once again as one incredible design follows another.

If our thinking apprentice continues to work with visual images, he becomes his own creative artist, perhaps a genius in form, design and colour. If he gradually exchanges the visual medium for the conceptual, he may become the philosopher.

But he could just as easily exchange the visual for the mathematical or scientific concept to master these fields instead.

And each will offer him its own field of wisdom, its own particular challenge to creativity. By whatever path, as he aspires towards the spiritual, the once-apprentice-thinker becomes the sage, the visionary. Such vision in its highest and truest form is indeed all too rare.

To make a tangible and worthwhile contribution in this direction, is one of the aims and objects of Modern Spiritualism. Needless to say, Spiritualism, in common with all great movements of like nature, has met with its due share of criticism. Spiritualists, it is said, are the victims of their own imaginations. They claim to see what does not exist, painting with their minds pictures they wish to see. They are people who hear silence and give to emptiness shape, colour and form.

Before we rush to reply to our critics, it may be a good thing to remind them (as well as ourselves) of Colton's words, "Men were born with two eyes and but one tongue, in order that they should see twice as much as they say."

Vision is, in its highest sense, dependent upon the physical act of seeing and upon all human emotional, psychic, mental and spiritual faculties to varying extents.

Seeing, complex and wonderful though it may be, is but a small part of the larger operation of vision. Vision requires not only that you see, but also that you feel and respond. It requires you to feel and respond with the full totality of the physical, mental, psychic, emotional and spiritual self.

So often what many of our critics and fellow Spiritualists permit themselves is not vision at all, but a brief glimpse or peep. Their perception, their response, their understanding is incomplete. Hence the all too rash and harsh judgements of man. Hence too the frustrating confusion and bewilderment of men who do not know if reality is life or dream.

Let us start with ourselves, and become aware of how our perception is incomplete. Once we know that, we can attempt to deepen it, extend it, make it whole.

Even physical seeing is incomplete. One of the methods which helps us to enter a fuller world of vision is what we might call comparative seeing. We see more clearly when we can compare what we are seeing with something we have already seen.

Acceptance of the fact that "I am," or understanding of this to be this, and that to be that, is only possible because of our ability to compare. The difference or contrast gives to each object a reality and individuality of its own.

Thus brightness has a particular meaning to us as distinct from darkness, but only because we have the ability to see the difference between the two states. Because of our ability to contrast, we are able to see more clearly.

Now, comparisons are made not only with things which can be seen in the strict physical or objective sense. Objective seeing is, after all, very limited in its scope. For something to become really meaningful to you, your seeing it in the physical or objective sense must have some degree of confirmation from at least one other of the senses. These senses are much more closely linked with seeing than is generally assumed, not least because each delivers messages to us which have to be interpreted by us before they mean anything at all.

Seeing is rarely believing until some other sense confirms that sight. We look and see the object. But do we see...or do we imagine? We do not — and cannot know — unless there is confirmation from another sense. Can we also feel this object, or hear it, taste or smell it? If the answer is yes, confirmation by one or more of our other senses gives to seeing a new degree of reality and significance.

We need contrast to see clearly. We need confirmation to see more clearly still. But objective seeing — even at its vivid best — still only takes us to the shallow waters of life. By this method, we are brought only to touch the surface or appearance of things. To become truly alive, to embrace and be embraced by reality, to be immersed in the deeper waters of awareness, we must be able to use our subjective faculties of seeing, sensing, hearing and feeling. We must become aware of our power within. We must see with that inner power.

Each of our physical senses has its psychic counterpart. And with the awakening of these psychic senses, the whole range and function of comparative analysis becomes greatly enlarged. The terms for these senses are often bandied about, and not always accurately used. However, seeing with the inner eye may be called clairvoyance. Hearing psychically is clairaudience. Feeling, tasting, smelling come under the title clairsentience.

The psychic senses are more fully developed in some than in others, but in all they are sensitive first to nature around us, then to people we come in contact with. As they develop further, this awareness extends to spirit people and the spirit world. Gradually (in this life or another) these same senses will learn to perceive qualities of the more highly developed soul, until awareness of God is their gift.

All physical matter, inert and alive, is a shorthand expression of the power of spirit. We seek first to see the symbol, then to identify it, then to unfold its significance. Our vision of the physical helps us to begin that search for understanding. And if ever we see and truly understand the message of physical creation, we may venture to take the next step of seeing beyond the physical - to look psychically at the spiritual nature we guessed at from the physical. In using these psychic senses, first we offer ourselves a further set of contrasts. These make both the physical and the spiritual more understandable, and secondly offer a new kind of confirmation to our first look at an object, person or experience.

To use both sets of awakened senses is a major breakthrough towards that higher degree of seeing which is called perception or understanding. It is at this point that you instinctively feel that although as yet you do not know, you are going to know soon. You may not yet understand, but already you see that path along which (in due time) you will find understanding.

It is therefore unfair of a critic to censure others for having an ability to perceive which is not yet his. The critic has not within himself the faculty to provide confirmation of their experience. It is equally unfair of a Spiritualist to claim mastery of such higher perception when he has only glimpsed its possibilities.

These glimpsed possibilities promise to be hugely satisfying, but they can only be accepted at great cost. The cost is the abandoning of conventional thinking and the adopting of what you might like to call an alternative world view. Now many people are interested in the new and the alternative, but today they are going to look for this view with their physical senses, they are going to ask to experience it with their physical selves...and they will not be able to do so. In consequence, their disappointment will find its expression against those who (if you like) insist that the Emperor's New Clothes are real, despite what the objectivity of their physical senses might tell them.

The man who sees with his eyes and his soul, step by step will learn to tread the path of acceptance. He will accept that he exists, that he sees, hears and feels. His subjective awareness will enable him to accept that there are things which are good, and those which are not. But he will also have to learn to accept restriction.

As he finds himself engaged in the struggle to absorb and retain the things of life which are good, and reject those which are not, he will learn that often the things he wishes to accept can only be obtained at the price of enduring what he would wish to reject.

Human society is fraught with the confusion and frustration of conflicting individual desires. To survive in some recognisable form, the will or law of society will often override the desire, hope or dream of man the individual. Individual man soon finds that his own degree of power to accept what he wants in his life, is strictly limited.

Firstly, it is limited by the laws of Nature: he may desire eternal youth and good health, but as the years pass, he will inevitably be offered age and precarious health. Nature's laws exist, and there is no alternative but to accept them.

Secondly, the laws of society will limit him. A man may wish to live in comfort, or have three wives. He may steal to provide his desired life style; he may marry all three of his loves; but his life will not be problem-free, for he shall have to pay the price decided by society - imprisonment, ostracism, or whatever.

It is true that the laws of Nature can be so used and exploited to such an advantage as to assist in the growth and evolution of man. It is also true that man the individual can, by his own efforts and example, do much to modify and improve the laws of society, but success in these directions is determined by the degree of vision or new awareness which can be aroused. However, man is but an individual, and society is a collective. There are many barriers which hinder and prevent the acceptance of his vision.

Besides this, man is ever torn between the conflicting desires of wanting to be himself (with his own essence, his own skill and

93

talent) and at the same time wanting to belong. He wants to be accepted as a part of his people, to be one of the herd, to be a member of society.

It is all too easy then to reject the new truth, to cast aside the progressive idea, because it does not conform to the fashion of the moment. Scorn, ridicule and even contemptuous abuse, is considered by many, far too high a price for the acceptance of a new truth.

So far as society as a whole is concerned, the simple truth of Spiritualism is rejected. It is rejected because its critics lack the vision to perceive its truth, and it remains rejected because Spiritualists who have glimpsed its truth have lacked the vision to perceive that truth more extensively.

Some people won't accept Spiritualism because their standing in society would suffer in consequence. Some are content and happy in their ignorance. Death has so long been considered an occasion for mourning and grief that others cling to it as an opportunity for sorrow and will not thank you for depriving them of it. Others still cannot admit that their previous opinion was wrong. A further group simply haven't seen Spiritualism working effectively... if it doesn't seem to work, why try to use it?

But with vision, these objections melt away.

There are always those with a deep and genuine grief, who are filled with strong and powerful desires for more knowledge concerning death. And again, there are those who are aware that their scientific, philosophical and religious knowledge is incomplete, and earnest desire to know more regarding the laws and fuller implications of death.

It is to these honest desires that the Spirit World can most readily respond. And it is in these directions that Spiritualism could more effectively pursue its efforts. To these people, Spiritualism can teach that the first function of vision is to bring to them the awareness of the ever-evolving, ever-extending nature of human perception. It can teach man to acknowledge the reality which abides beyond the range of his normal physical senses.

To this end, physical phenomena are used by Spirit intelligences to attract man's attention to the fact of survival. These phenomena, although physical in nature, nevertheless quite clearly indicate a state or order of being beyond the physical state. Acceptance of this fact is the first great step towards understanding the tremendous difference between seeing and vision.

Vision of beings, orders and states not seen is possible. This knowledge brings a new and richer sense of awareness. It is a higher form of knowing. It teaches us that life is more meaningful and altogether more full of colour than ever we had dreamt. Perception is given a new height, breadth and depth.

Manifestations through the power of physical mediumship are rarer today than they were in the past. Their very rarity makes people more interested in sharing the experience of them now. Such manifestations serve a wonderful purpose, but they should not be confused with the essence of Spiritualism: they should never be regarded as permanent means of communion. This method is only the knocking on the wall. It is the call of Spirit to attract our attention. It brings to our notice the fact of Spiritual reality.

Now when the reality of true spirit communion has truly been established, these cumbersome methods which restrict the style of spirit, are replaced by the more natural and direct approaches to our psychic and spiritual faculties. It is by these means that Spiritual laws can be used to much greater effect.

One of the first effects of this higher vision which gradually results from communion with the Spirit World, is vision of the very great difference in the laws and values between spirit and earth states of being. As our psychic and spiritual faculties become tuned to this higher degree of consciousness, it can be seen that our understanding of physical laws is very much of a temporal and artificial nature. Clearer understanding and vision are only possible when these temporal conceptions are replaced by the more permanent and higher forms of knowledge which are made available by spirit communion.

This means that things we call truths today are only true in the light of our limited understanding. Tomorrow, with further insight and understanding, they may cease to be true. We must be brave enough to accept this. Einstein's work showed that Newtonian physics only applied within a certain scale: they were true, but within limitations. Chaos theory today throws doubt on time, place, pattern and predictability. Our truths must grow with our perception, our vision.

They can only do this while we retain the faculty to dream. If we understand that perception within each individual has the potential to evolve continually, then we open up the possibility of growing, evolving truth. A truth whose discovery is enhanced by communion with spirit, and made possible by our ability to dream beyond our present experience and understanding.

We can perceive beyond our present state. Quite obviously, when we make contact with beings of another state, we expect to find certain differences. In fact, if such differences cannot be found, then we may have good reason to doubt if we are making true contact. It is these differences which make us look again at some of our previous conceptions, and to examine afresh the biases and limitations of much of our earthly knowledge.

Let me take an example: for many years, the law of cause and effect was considered as a reliable basis for our conclusions. But gradually, this law became suspect because experience began to show that what we assumed to be the same cause, did not always come out with the same effect.

However, psychic and spiritual awareness can show that it is not the law of cause and effect which is at fault. Rather it is our perception of it. Conclusions based on human perception alone must always be suspect. The range of human perception is dependent upon our degree of alertness and sensitivity. When we make an attempt to explain a series of events, we say,"A was the cause and B was the effect." But in truth, all we see is what is apparent to our limited powers of observation.

All the while, parts of the effect which we do not see, continue to build up, and suddenly the build-up of these undetected causes explodes, and we see effects which were totally unexpected. Our imperfect vision thus provides us with many surprises. The more perfect our vision, the less likely we are to be taken unawares by circumstances.

At a very basic level, the humble fortune teller perceives with her non-physical senses (i.e. with her psychic senses) and can therefore predict the future (or a likely future) with greater ease than the objective materialist. There is nothing stranger in this than the gambler who is aware of 'form' placing more winning bets than he could make by purely random choice. The man with access to statistical information about (say) Britain's population will be able to make more accurate predictions about the number of jobs required in ten years' time, than the man with no such information. Such 'vision' promotes understanding.

It soon becomes clear then, that communion with the World of Spirit, and the exercise of psychic and spiritual faculties, greatly extends the power of human perception. Slowly, the truth unfolds...it is not the medium or the Spiritualist who is the victim of hallucination; not the Spiritualist who is the dreamer of dreams; nor is it the medium who is trapped in the world of illusion...such people (properly trained) simply see further and in more detail.

The truth is that it is the critic's loud voice which deafens him to the softer voice of truth. It is his imagined ability to see the truth which has blinded him to the reality of life. In the end, it is the medium who is able to reveal that death is the cause not of oblivion, but of a fuller and greater state of life.

Extended vision allows us to see cause and effect in a different light. It also encourages a wider view of space and time. Now, we would expect to find that the values of space and time are different in the World of Spirit. If you think about it, each state or kingdom has a set of space and time values of its own. In the mineral kingdom, millions of years are sometimes required for just one change. The vegetable kingdom at times requires only a few months to make manifest a complete change in its mode of function and appearance. In contrast, in the human kingdom, three score years and ten traditionally cover the whole cycle of human unfoldment.

In other words, time is a myth. The saying that time heals is a fallacy. Time by its nature does nothing. The event is the reality, and time only the container or the environment of the the event.

Now, those who wish to teach psychic or spiritual unfoldment are here held in question. For the requirements of spirit are not calendar date or time as measured by the clock, but 'time' as determined by the intensity and purity of desire and purpose. The correct time for spirit communion is as and when there is a desire to absorb, and the ability to use, the revelation of the spirit.

People sometimes talk of the astral plane as the one we

experience in going to spirit. The astral body we shall then inhabit is commonly called the desire body. What does this mean? It means that, freed from the restriction of the cumbersome physical body, our souls — clothed in a lighter vehicle — will be moved by their desires. In other words, you will be where you want to be for as long as you want it.

This sort of experience could be very traumatic at first, because in the consumer-led culture of the late twentieth century, we are encouraged to want continually: to want activity, novelty, change, variety: and to want quickly. To transfer this level of superficial but powerful desiring to the astral plane would lead us all into a frenzied activity akin to madness where time was determined by the rate of change of desire. This helps to explain why we have to rest awhile in the etheric: a plane closer in nature to that of the Earth.

Greater vision tells us that space is mythical too. As time is the encasement of the event or experience, so space is the encasement of the object. In the higher reality of extended vision, both time and space are boundless and without limit. Yet both are vital requirements of creative life.

Here again we see that it is the Spiritualist who becomes alert and alive to the truth and reality of life. Vision which enters into its true and natural field with the inflow of spiritual awareness, reveals that time does not age, wear or restrict us. Neither need we be the victims or servants of an artificial and temporal understanding of space. "There's No Such Thing As Far Away" is the title of one of Richard Bach's books. Spiritually, we know this to be true. Telepathy demonstrates it, clairvoyance reinforces it. With extended vision, we are where we want to be. The visionary has no prison cell simply because he sees beyond it: he is free. Likewise, when you are spiritually free, there is literally freedom in chains.

The great difference between spirit life as compared with earth life, is that spirit can dispense with the restrictions and limitations of temporal values. Their growth and change is determined not by the passage of time, but by the intensity of their desire. The means of their flight is concerned only with the force or power of their wills.

It was the intensity of his desire to understand that produced

Jesus' vision of truth which caused him to proclaim long ago, "I and the Father are one."

This was his symbolic way of saying "The law is, and I am of the law. I and the law are one."

Our principles of Fatherhood and Brotherhood are but a reaching out in an endeavour to embrace the same eternal truth. Spirit is the positive, active, aspect of law. It is life. We are spirit, so Brotherhood in its fullest sense becomes the brotherhood of all life.

Clear vision acknowledges the differences between spirit and earth life. A clear seer makes effective use of this knowledge.

But it is equally important that we should, in communion with our spirit friends, find areas of similarity too. Without this degree of similarity, much of our communion would become meaningless, and would fail in the important function of providing evidence of spirit return. It would fail, because without some continuing similarity between incarnate and discarnate spirit people, anything they wished to convey to us would be incomprehensible to us.

Happily, the distinctive personality of the human spirit continues. The sense of humour, phraseology, likes and dislikes, memories, hopes and feelings : all the traits which made the human being the one we loved: these continue. And although with progress their environment ceases to be in exact parallel to that of earth's, and their freedoms are enhanced, all the drives to think and hope and feel, to create, express, improve and discover: all these things are the same. They are comprehensible to us as stages and activities upon the pathway to God. Primarily, it is this colour or thumb print of human character and personality which survives physical death. This evidence of personality is the authority which places its stamp upon every genuine and worthwhile communion.

Such worthwhile communion will not fail to inspire the degree of vision we so desperately need today. This is the vision which must and will illuminate the seance room, and give new life and lustre to the whole structure and form of Spiritualism's presentation.

Conversation is important to human relationships. Equally it is important that we converse with the friends of the spirit world.

There can be no question that conversation with each other can be both enjoyable and helpful. But this should no be confused with communion.

Of course, it is good for us that on occasion we "make a gladsome noise unto the Lord." By all means clap your hands, sound your trumpet, clash your cymbals and bang your drums. Most certainly it is good that at times you should really let yourselves go. It is good to be roused and to allow ourselves to become emotionally tipsy.

But again, do not confuse this with spiritual awareness. For the Psalmist said,"Be still." Silence has an eloquence of its own. "Let us be silent," said Emerson, "that we may hear the whispers of the gods."

Silence is the womb of vision. Thought mingles with thought, and soul with soul becomes eternally, closely entwined. Vision breathes the air of pure ecstasy. By time it is untouched. By space it is not imprisoned or confined.

The cry goes up, "Let us give Spiritualists a new image!" Why bruise and vainly exhaust yourselves in trying to change the unchangeable?

We need to strip away the clouds of misunderstanding and confusion. Those who are inclined to the belief of Theosophy, astrology, phrenology or numerology have a right to state their case. But let their cause be stated from their own platforms and soapboxes. Those who claim they can foretell your future and give readings of your fortunes or misfortunes have every right to practise their professed talents. But let them do so in their private rooms, their seaside tents or arcade shops. The platform and seance room of Spiritualism should concern itself with proclaiming and demonstrating its own important truths.

We have handicaps still in the proclamation of our own simple truths. The greatest restrictions to our progress are:

1. Deliberate fraud.
2. Unconscious fraud
3. Inferior mediumship
4. Weak presentation in seance room and church service

Concerning deliberate fraud, I don't think we need to worry unduly. There is little motivation for fraud amongst mediums whose work is by and large concerned with serving churches. Their fees are traditionally small, and if church committees are dissatisfied with their work, they will simply not ask them back again. Mediums who are highly paid and famous for their stage presentations are very few and far between. If they succumb to fraud, the media will be all too eager to uncover it and consequently to end their careers.

A further motivation for fraud might be to influence other people. Any medium who seeks to influence strongly the attitudes or actions of his sitter is bound to be suspect to any thinking Spiritualist, for the very reason that Spiritualism itself teaches that our actions and thoughts are our own personal responsibility: such is spiritual law. Anyone who blindly follows another, however inspired or charismatic that other may be, is acting irresponsibly. He is duty bound to think about and question all that is placed before him. If he does this, there is at least a counterbalance to the kind of fraud motivated by the desire to influence.

At its very simplest, unless a medium can provide evidence of survival of death to a sitter, the mediumship should be seriously held in question, belief suspended. Now the phrase "suspension of belief" is important. Condemnation of a medium who has failed to satisfy is never constructive or positive. Lack of evidence today may not mean that there will never be any evidence: that time may come. But until it does come the sitter should not assume that the person he is sitting with has the gift of mediumship that they would like to claim. The sitter should then respond to the 'medium' accordingly.

More often than not, then, the deliberate fraud is soon seen for what he is. In any case, when the standard of mediumship is raised to the superior levels which are possible, the fraud just will not be able to compete. It is with the unconscious fraud and the inferior medium that the greatest harm is done.

Both the unconscious fraud and the inferior medium often have quite genuine psychic talent, but seem unwilling to pay the price of natural psychic and spiritual unfoldment. The result is that we are given in the name of mediumship some fragment of psychic or spiritual contact, plus a stream of illusions which spring from the unconscious mind of the medium. This is the result of limited

101

vision.

With the true vision of what really is possible, Spiritualists should agree upon required standards of mediumship in the seance room. And only when these highest standards are achieved, should mediumship be allowed to reflect itself into the church service, public demonstration, or other areas of society where mediumship might with advantage be used.

Mediumship requires refinement. Spiritualists whose vision should be their gift to society, have allowed their vision to become colourless and obscure. They have become slaves to the confused mood and bewildering tempo of their age. Whereas methods of mass production may serve industry well, they cannot serve the seance room. These are not the methods of spiritual unfoldment.

To attend a church service this week, be invited to sit for unfoldment the following seek, and the next week be asked to conduct the service, is not and cannot be the way to obtain a healthy, progressive and strong presentation. Only when the medium has grown, has become aware of his growth and has attempted to understand the significance of his increased closeness to spirit, can he hope to have the strength of presentation required. Only when he knows how he has grown, can he hope to grow further still and help others in their progression.

How can we judge mediumship? What standards would we set? We cannot stress too strongly the naturalness of mediumship and spiritual communion. Anything which is suggestive of being unnatural should immediately be suspect. All forms of trance, control and communion should be natural. Whenever they are not so, either the sitter, the medium or the spirit is at fault, and corrective measures should at once be taken.

The spiritual embrace meant to induce trance, control or an inspired state, should not result in a condition of shivering and shaking, moaning and groaning, which seems to suggest that the medium is on his death bed, or is about to be executed. Whenever we hear a voice from Spirit, we expect it at least to be in some way similar to the voice when on earth. We do not expect a dry, hard, eerie voice more in keeping with what we would associate with the most ancient monasteries or a comedy version of a haunted house: away with all of that!

102

Each man is unique. Quite apart from all physical differences, every man has a degree of talent and emotional warmth; a shade of character and personality which is his own. It is by the individual's uniqueness and without any mistakes that he can be recognised when he communicates through a medium. This evidence of uniqueness is what we are looking for in our mediumship. We are looking for simplicity and clarity of presentation. We are looking for an understanding of why the communication is taking place. We are looking for a mediumship which encourages sitters to become aware of their own spiritual potential.

Spiritualism at its best is a truth of vision — vision alert and positive. It gives meaning, scope and ability to the soul. All strata of life become openly interfused and are touched by divinity when viewed with the more full understanding. The eyes of the soul become open so that the poet can say that man's heightened awareness has "A sense sublime of something far more gently interfused, whose dwelling is the light of setting suns, and the blue sky, the round ocean, the living air and in the mind of man. A motion and a spirit that impels and rolls though all things."

Chapter Twelve

INSPIRATION AND PERSPIRATION

THE South Wales Summer School started as an annual event in 1945. It took Tom and Mabel Hibbs many years to ask me (a Welshman!) to lecture there. This I did, and became deeply involved with the school from then on, making many remarkable friends through it.

The first lecture I gave was "Unfolding Consciousness" in 1951. The District Council Summer School was a prestigious event so I was anxious to do my best. I wrote out the entire lecture in longhand, memorised it and made notes. Such very thorough preparation, but a good discipline.

I spoke at the Summer School every year after that so cannot have done too badly on my first attempt after all! Milestones of Philosophy followed in 1952. Then came Interpenetrative Philosophy (1953), Soul Perception (1954), The Eternal Theme (1955), Man and the Infinite (1956), Spiritual Development (1957), Inspiration (1958), Communion (1959) and Natural Philosophy (1960). In the 60s I delivered The Human Machine, Spiritualism in the Modern World, Vision, and several others which Kate has since spring cleaned into oblivion! It was a demanding and stimulating time.

It is these lectures that have been woven into the fabric of this book.

As I learned after the preparation of that first lecture, inspiration never comes out of the blue. It is a favourite saying of mine that inspiration is "99 per cent perspiration". It is that extra 1 per cent which makes it all worth while, and draws the whole idea into clearer focus. The inspired mind is the hard working mind, the one that prepares in every possible way it can before inspiration can strike.

There is no glamorous, mysterious or mystical explanation: it's just hard work!

Chapter Thirteen

INSPIRATION

WHEN an idea pops into mind and it solves the problem you have been struggling with, you have a hunch or gamble successfully, it's often described as inspiration. You were inspired.

Similarly, when someone stands up and gives a talk with no previous preparation, except perhaps the calming of the mind, you might say he was an inspirational speaker.

Well, I would disagree with you. I would disagree because I see inspiration as the blessing of knowledge we receive when we touch the highest level we are capable of reaching. It is virtually the experience of God.

Now the inspiration of the savage will be very different from that of the sage. And the inspiration you are capable of today, may be much more lowly than what you may achieve in your later years. Yet if you receive it, the experience will be one of the most significant in your life. It won't be on the level of a hunch or a lucky gamble.

Spiritualists, in their enthusiasm, are prone to using "inspiration" more glibly than they perhaps should. It is important to realise that the impressions and guidance received from Spirit are not necessarily of the highest quality...no more than I would expect your helpful advice to a friend to be inspired from on high. The help we receive from Spirit is just that — help. It needn't be spiritual, hugely moving or revelatory: it is just useful at the time. The recipient should be grateful for that, but if he has a respect for words, he will not call it inspiration.

One of the advantages of age is that you can quote the length of your vast experience to others! So making use of my advantage,

I shall say that over my sixty years' experience of mediumship and spiritual work, this is what I have learned about inspiration — in the true sense of the word.

This land of inspiration is no lazy man's paradise. It does not, it cannot, it will not, arrive free of charge. Be it soon or late, we have to learn that, as I have already said, perspiration is the currency of inspiration. And when we would stand outside this gateway of inspiration, we will need a key to unlock the gate. There is only one key, and the key is self.

We commence our enquiry with self because in the first instance, it is Self which must be primarily concerned with inspiration. Our first task is to understand that which is to be inspired rather than looking at that which inspires. Indeed, a golden maxim well worth remembering throughout this enquiry is that God helps those who help themselves.

Unless you are sure and steady in your self, your belief or faith in other men, in a higher power or in God, will be a vulnerable, unsteady faith easily buffeted by life's harsher circumstances. If you will not — or cannot — look honestly at yourself, you can never honestly believe in others. So before inspiration can occur, there must come a moment in your life when your self becomes ruthlessly aware of your self. Then you will realise that all envy is ignorance, and all imitation is suicide. Nothing can alter the fact that you are you — for better or for worse. You must learn bravely to express the power of your self, and with healthy buoyancy and confidence declare that you will be true to your self to the fullest of your ability. No-one can do it better than you!

This requires courage. The first demand of this approach is that you should conform to no system of ideas: no "ism," no party tradition where it departs from your own belief and understanding. The second is that you should trust yourself. You should learn to express the power of your own self and know that the eternal is stirring in your heart, working through your hand, and would radiate its august power through your whole being.

At the headquarters of all our action, there is a mind. Now the mind belongs to the psychic aspect of the universe, and is not to be explained or defined physically. All our actions, every thought, notion or dream, can only function with the consent of the mind.

In the same way, a certain energy, lust or passion (if it is to be suppressed or redirected) can only be so at the wish or pleasure of the mind. The mind is the dreamer of dreams. The wish or pleasure of the mind makes us into the artist, the poet, the architect, the builder — makes us the constant recipient of consciousness.

We are likened to a vast, limitless sea of unconsciousness. The mind, from this fount of unconsciousness, is receiving continually from all parts of this boundless universe of worlds. Therefore the consciousness is having piped into it parts of this boundless reservoir of unconsciousness. The nature of that part is determined by the particular call which is sent out by any one of our many emotional nerve centres. These in turn are influenced by circumstance and environment.

In other chapters, we have considered sensation, and the mind becoming aware of sensation. This is what I call a degree of uncontrolled consciousness. In other words, consciousness has been brought into being by the chance influence of circumstance and environment. The ego is slow to assert itself. It will only bestir itself from its complacent sleep state as a result of intensified pressure, desire or demand from the emotional, feeling self. It is generally at this stage, when our emotions or desires meet with some form of friction, that we protest at the possibility of defeat until the ego becomes aroused.

When it becomes aroused, the ego takes stock of the situation and by making heavier demands upon the unconscious, or redirecting the emotional desire, usually succeeds in establishing a condition of peace once more.

Failure to do so causes the ego to hold an inquest. In such an inquest, it sheds its beam upon the limitations of the total self. Through the experience of such inquests, the intellect gradually evolves into being. Now it is the function of the well-trained intellect to direct experience and knowledge into the unconscious until, at some future moment, it can be called up again to serve efficiently and effectively the needs of the conscious self.

If no deliberate attempt is made to decide the nature or the quality of that which the unconscious is to absorb, then we shall not be in a position to decide the nature or quality of what is to pour forth into the conscious, or what will be transformed into word or deed at some later date. Inspiration has to be carefully prepared for. The first thing you have to prepare is your self.

Having prepared it, you must not limit it. Once the intellect has awakened from its slumber, its constant analysis and evaluation often results in us living with too small a portion of our real selves. What we have to realise is this: that each one of our emotional nerve centres is a potential source of energy. These sources of energy are not only transferrable; they also come under the will and direction of the ego and can be merged into one absolute state of completeness.

This is the main difference between words and actions of mediocrity and words and actions of true greatness and genius. Heights of greatness can be reached by the ability of the ego to call upon and direct the entire wealth and totality of our inherent sources of energy and power.

It is then that you first glimpse the faint shadow of inspiration. It is here that you can stand and gaze with amazement at the achievements of your own efforts, listen enthralled at the words which pour forth from your own mouth, gaze unbelievingly on the work of your own hands.

Spiritualism can lead us to a clearer and fuller understanding of inspiration. Let me unfold these thoughts a little.

The common notion of inspiration is embodied in a picture something like this. An author sits at his desk with a blank sheet of paper in front of him. He cannot think what to write. Then all of a sudden inspiration strikes — and the words flow from his pen.

The Spiritualist version of this would be that a spirit draws close to him while he gazes blankly at the paper, and dictates what should be written, takes over his arm (as in automatic writing), or impresses him with a vision which he then expresses in words.

Now poets, artists and even scientists and philosophers have claimed to have their inspiring "muses" to aid them in their work — and the work sounds pleasant and effortless. Similarly there are, even today, people who can claim their books have been produced through automatic writing or overshadowing. I shall not argue with that, but I shall pose a question or two.

Firstly I shall ask: "Is the end product up to your normal standard? Is it the sort of thing you could personally produce without any further help from anyone?" If the answer is, "No, it is not as good as I would do myself," then my reply would be along the lines that they are wasting their time. They should rely on their own natural wit and skill.

If the answer is,"Yes, it is just as good as I can produce myself," then I must ask a further question, "What makes you think it is inspired then?"

But if the answer is, "Oh, it is far different (or much better) than I could do myself alone," then I would consider the possibility of inspiration. If their production was beyond their knowledge altogether, then I would be more inclined to think that the work was achieved through trance or very heavy overshadowing rather than inspiration. The major difference between the two is that in trance the medium allows himself to be physically taken over by the spirit, and his own consciousness is kept to a minimum. In inspiration, the consciousness of the inspired is heightened to the maximum degree.

With some commonsense questions, and a little understanding born of Spiritualism, we can begin to understand what is not inspiration. The same approach can also help us to understand what is inspiration. Much of the philosophy received through mediumship reflects the age-old teachings of (for example) the Indian and Chinese cultures. So the understanding that Spiritualists have today is not necessarily new, and is none the worse of that.

Think of space. But don't think of it as empty. Think of it as pulsing with energy which is on the verge of patterning itself into a manifestation of some sort. Maybe the energy will become sound, light, heat, mass or an idea. The potential of this space is unlimited.

Now think of something else. When did you last see a Radio One programme pass you by or a television advert before it was there on your screen? You never do, of course, yet the signals are travelling through space all the time. You, on your own, can never spot them, but they are there all the same. So in amongst the space which is full of potential, there will also be signals: patterns to be made sense of if only you have the right kind of receiver.

Now imagine this. I am thinking of something very ordinary, say a plate of beans on toast. That idea is nothing more than a pattern of mental energy and as such will ripple through space much as ripples in a pool extend out from their source. That mundane thought will continue to exist in the universal space we have been considering.

Now, if my daughter should suddenly turn round and say, "Fancy some beans on toast, Dad?" I should not be surprised for she has done nothing more than catch the idle thought of the moment. That is basically how telepathy works. The reason she catches it is because she is thinking about what to have for tea, and her unspoken question attracts my unspoken reply.

We have objective evidence to prove that telepathy does exist so Spiritualist philosophy may not be so far from the truth when it teaches that the boundless space around us is woven through with every thought ever generated and that the only thing we need to do to gain access to such thought is to ask a question relevant to it. The Biblical saying, "Ask and it shall be given," makes so much more sense then, doesn't it?

The way this philosophy is generally expressed is that thoughts are living things, and if we wish to gain further understanding, we should learn to attune ourselves to the Universal Mind (all those ideas we were talking about). So the easy way to inspiration would seem to be:

To tune into the Universal Mind and to ask it a question. The answer will come flooding back. And you, the recipient, will be inspired.

Of course, there's always a snag, isn't there? The snags here are: how do you tune in, how do you receive the answer, and will you understand the answer once you have received it? It is these questions which make inspiration so difficult and so rare.

However, for the moment, suffice to say that Spiritualist philosophy declares that because your mind is not a physical entity, and because the ideas it produces are living patterns of energy which continue to exist in space, it is possible for the individual to gain access to ideas and understanding beyond his normal experience.

Now, it seems to me psychologists have yet to recognise the true nature of the mind. Until such can be confident that the mind is more than the function of the physical brain, they will find the phenomenon of inspiration impossible to understand.

The wide and varied experience of astral travel and out-of-the-body experiences, coupled with telepathy, prediction, far seeing and mediumship, will surely, eventually, provide such a substantial body of evidence for the scientists of the mind that they will be able to follow where the facts lead them: to the conclusion that mind functions beyond the body and is not dependent upon it. Then hopefully they will begin to see the reality of inspiration and will work on releasing its untold potential for the good of the world.

The content of inspiration already exists in the collective unconsciousness, or the Universal Mind. Having ideas, expressing them in some form, trying to understand things — that is what people do. Those are the functions of man's consciousness. If other beings have consciousness, their thoughts too will be in the universal mind, but we may not (as yet) have the ability to recognise much less than understand them. If God or higher beings than ourselves have thoughts, we may not be able to understand their form or content either.

Whatever it is we are trying to understand exists before we attempt to understand it. It has a pattern or principle even if we cannot identify it. So when our inspiration comes, the idea is not a new one. It is new only to us, and is original only in the way we express it. What do I mean by that?

Well, let's take Pythagoras and his theorem. Before ever he thought about it, the sum of the squares of the two sides equalled the square of the hypotenuse of every triangle. Its reality existed before he expressed his theorem. No doubt when he did first expound his discovery, men were amazed at the reality he opened up to them, but he only discovered and expressed it — he did not invent it. It is the case with any idea we may have which is not directly creative. The reality was there first. Put a different way, that means that all man's inspiration is drawn from the womb of the unconscious or the universal mind.

Can man have a truly creative idea, or is that strictly the realm for God? All around us we can see items made by man, and systems devised by him which did not exist before. He would seem to have the power of originality. What he cannot do is generate a principle, a rule by which the universe works. The conclusion I draw then is

Even though the photo on the left was taken decades ago, it is undoubtedly Will Ford, pictured above as he is today.

Flashback to yesteryear and members of the Spiritualists' National Union's South Wales District Council. Here Will Ford (top left) appears with F. Lowe, A. Jones, S. Rees, Mrs M. Hibbs, G. Harris, G. Dally and I. Davies.

Will Ford with his wife Kate and (left) with daughter Ann.

How the years roll by! Here Will Ford (right) is seen with his best friend, Marsden.

The South Wales Summerschool in Penarth in the early 60s.

Here Will Ford is seen with Linda Muir

that man can be inspired to understand and discover the essential nature of the universe, and with or without inspiration, he can use his understanding to make an original expression of it. His original expression may be a work of art or a practical invention.

Inspiration, then, is the drawing out of the womb of the great unconscious, the very highest of truths.

He who wishes to be inspired must learn first his oneness with universal life. Individuals of true greatness are the first to acknowledge that they have a debt to other men. The artist will always need his model and his critic, the poet his subject and his listener. The playwright and the musician — the orator too — require the performer, the audience, the event, the occasion. All life will insist on earning its own place in the scoring. Thus is equilibrium born to the universe, and humanity is given poise. Where there is a generator, there has to be a receiver or the efforts of the first are in vain.

But this interdependency exists at the initial stage too. Before man can make the creation, he has to have the understanding and the inspiration. What seen and unseen helpers made the understanding feasible? Sharing and co-operation is required at this level too. And when discovery of a principle or a high truth is made, what then?

Once again, help has been at hand, for the very universe of which you are a part becomes (in the inspired moment) a part of you as you experience your revelation. In every aspect of discovery and creativity, the individual opens himself to his universe and exchanges his effort and diligence for a glimpse of its truth. Without the sense and experience of oneness with the universe, there can be no real inspiration.

Mediumship requires individual effort on the part of the medium as well as co-operation with and receptivity to Spirit. If people in general would rid themselves of the idea that mediumship is something restricted to the seance or circle, they would understand it a great deal better.

Inspiration is, of course, the highest form of mediumship. Yet how many people would acknowledge that the greatest thinkers, leaders, inventors of our day and of history were mediums? They would not consider it for a moment. Ah, but if they would consider it, identify it, study it and train for it, how much greater and higher might the discoveries and inventions be? Men could identify the mechanism for releasing and achieving their potential.

The reason few people do not consider mystics, artists, scientists, etc., to be mediums is because they have been led to believe (as no doubt many Spiritualists do) that the aim of mediumship is solely to prove the survival of the human personality in an afterlife.

This would be to restrict it unbearably. It would be to leave man in the kindergarten when the high school and university of life beckoned. Yes, mediumship is intended to persuade man that he has a spirit, but it is also intended to motivate him or awaken him into using it.

Those with the task of developing potential mediums will usually begin by training them to be still. They will teach them first to still their bodies and then to still their minds.

This does not mean that the medium will be a dozy, sleepy character. On the contrary, once the stillness is established, the trainee medium has to master the experience of a relaxed body and an alert but still mind. As clairvoyance develops, it is important that the medium's mind should not affect or colour what he is receiving. His task is to be receptive to the impressions he receives, and then to relay them as effectively as possible.

It is easy to think that to be a good medium, one should do absolutely nothing. However, that is not the case. One has to be still and receptive at the time, but preparation is essential and cannot be skimped if a higher mediumship is to be developed.

Inspiration is, like everything else in the universe, subject to law. I would implore those who are responsible for the training of mediums to stress the importance of the fact that inspiration does not just happen. Let us never be guilty of giving false encouragement to our students by telling them, "Just open your mouth and it will be filled." Let us remind them of the prayer, "Please God, help me to keep my big mouth shut until I know what I am talking about."

There is nothing magical or supernatural about the inflow of the power. It comes because the way has been made open for it, because the help of the prepared mind, the alertness of the ego and the will of the soul allows it to come. And because the correct preparation has been made.

Never be deceived into thinking that the importance of this preparation can be over-rated. Never believe that it is unnecessary. Of course, it is easy to be deceived: the air of spontaneity with which inspiration makes its appearance makes it all seem too easy. In some unguarded moment, we become receptive to an impulse or impression which spurs us on to a form of improvisation which excels our most carefully rehearsed efforts.

Many are the occasions when in vain we try to induce into the consciousness the thoughts and the words we need. Then, when all our attempts fail and we cease to do battle, there — fresh as the morning dew — calmly, unannounced, the thoughts appear. Don't be deceived: this gift is never free of charge. It comes because the trap has been set, because the price has already been paid. Our very inspiration has, in some other moment, been most carefully rehearsed.

What sort of thing am I talking about? If a medium wants to be a channel for more than the simple message of a name and a few identity traits, then a substantial vocabulary is important. How else could one convey specifically and effectively the information intended by Spirit?

The only alternative would be through a deep trance medium whose whole mechanism was taken over by the controlling spirit. From my experience, such a form of mediumship is extremely rare — and perhaps it is so rare because it is a mediumship which must involve a tremendous amount of effort from Spirit.

Most mediums should be able to contribute to, and help the flow of, information along. It is therefore important that the aspiring medium should exercise his mind and read. Do not be cajoled into believing that such reading is to allow you to "pad out" the communication: it is to make it brief, concise and professional. The medium is letting down his helpers and sitters if he aims for less than this.

If, of course, the medium reads about Spiritualism or philosophy, so much the better, because he will build up a fuller understanding of what he does. This means he will be able to explain it effectively to the very many people who have no idea at all of what he is doing, or how he does it, or indeed why he does it. The more information of this nature that the medium can offer, the more effective will be the essential message of Spiritualism.

The mind has to be induced to work. I have already suggested that the trainee medium read extensively as a means of preparation for his mediumship. There is another reason for this suggestion: it is to make the mind work. Mind is the latest development of man. It is the most modern part of his make-up. It is therefore the most lazy part of his being. Its most natural state is not wakefulness as might be imagined, but sleep or inertia.

Mind needs to be set tasks and induced into completing them. I am not suggesting that the medium should become a bookworm in order to make his mind work. This, too, has its dangers because he can easily over-read and cease to gain the benefit of his efforts. "Read a little, think a lot" is a good maxim. To turn over an idea in one's mind; to explore the various avenues it opens; to play devil's advocate with it: each of these is a simple exercise which encourages the mind to think and to increase its capacity for thought. This is the end-product we are aiming for. Once the medium has a great capacity for thought, he comes nearer the possibility of fine inspiration. It does not really matter what he learns to think about — as long as he learns to think!

Once he has learned to do so, he has to learn the control of that thought. Ironically, the greatest threat to the flow of inspiration lies within the consciousness itself, because it is the conscious thought which hinders the flow of the real genius. While the deeper depths of our unconscious yearns for life and a wider expression, our conscious mind, pleased with its achievements, its opinions, its "truths," often restricts the flow by analysis or self-doubt. It plays the part of Hamlet.

Although we have made tremendous progress in our ability to control the forces of nature, we are still so much in our infancy concerning the ability to control our own conscious thoughts. It is only with intense difficulty that we are able to concentrate on a given line of thought and seldom (if ever) that we meet with more than partial success. So often does the consciousness find itself at the mercy or under the influence of other personalities from our environment. So often it is distracted by the constant promptings from other parts of our own beings.

I suppose that is why some of the old bards were lovers of wine and tobacco. They were deliberately trying to lull the conscious state into a condition of inertia. That would make it possible for that part of their unconsciousness which was more suitable for the task in hand to perform its work without being unduly hindered by the conscious mind. The burning of incense, the playing of soft, solemn music at a religious service: these things are born of the same kind of motive.

But pure inspiration should need none of these artificial inducements. True greatness cannot be bought by a trick. It is true that such methods can result in work that will please and impress us. It is true that such works can entertain us, stir our imaginations, stimulate a degree of enthusiasm, but this is not the way the epic poem is written, or the work of immortal quality born. The deep sense of the profound which enraptures the soul and places its eternal finger on the heartbeat of the universe is something more than mechanical skill or technical ability. It is the true grandeur of the soul that is the cause.

Preparation does not stop with reading. It extends into being. A medium has to learn to be. He does this by the regular discipline of meditation: of taking time to sit quietly and learn to know himself, his real self. It is nothing new or original, of course, but meditation is effective. When a medium is working as (say) a clairvoyant, he directs his attention beyond himself to become aware of spirit presence.

In meditation, he uses the same skill of maintaining a still, alert mind, but this time he directs his attention inward — towards himself. This has a double benefit. First, it enables the man to understand himself. Secondly, it allows him to understand something of the nature of God (if we assume that each individual is a spark of God).

In understanding himself, he learns honesty. Meditation improves the man's awareness of the spiritual as well as of spirit. In making him spiritually aware, it begins to teach him of his true mission as a medium: to be a channel of teaching about the spiritual, about truth, about God. It is nothing less. But it also provides the necessary check to balance out the undoubted significance of his work.

117

Meditation truly undertaken has to make obvious to the practitioner that he is imperfect and vulnerable. In short, it teaches humility, essential to counterbalance the awesomeness of his task. Complete personal honesty is essential if he is to aim for truth: he will only have himself to blame if he is fooled or confused.

A footnote to all of this must be a reminder of the spiritual law "like attracts like." The best medium is the one who is the brightest, purest spirit, for he alone will be able to make contact with higher truth. If the lifestyle of the medium is suspect, if his motivation or behaviour is unsavoury, then it becomes impossible for him to reach above a certain spiritual level. We are told "Judge not lest ye be judged." We cannot truly judge another because we do not fully know them. This is why it is so important for the medium to be honest — for he has to be able to trust himself.

So preparation is all. Nearly all. We must not forget motivation. The only effective motivation for inspiration is love. It is the ever-evolving power of love, love which is pure, that induces the inspiration of truth.

Love comes in many forms. The artist may love an individual and find music, painting or poetry flowing through his soul. The philosopher and scientist might love truth just as ardently. The love of beauty or creation or God — each and all of these encourages the soul to breathe in truth beyond that which it knew before. To be inspired by anything else, or anything less, will colour the nature and form of the inspiration received.

"Love one another" is not really a command from a spiritual teacher. It is the only method by which the soul can grow. Those simple words form the complete operating instructions for the soul. There are no others.

But there is something else I would like to call to mind regarding our ability to be inspired. Have you ever noticed how the wisest people seem to have had the saddest lives? I don't mean that wisdom brings sadness. It doesn't. I mean that people who have had difficult lives are often wiser than those who have had smooth and untroubled ones.

People often ask if they are progressing along a spiritual path once they begin to be aware of their spiritual side. The simple answer is this, "If you've got problems, you're on the right path."

118

I don't say this flippantly. I say it because people progress through crisis. Why else do you think we all grow old and die in this life? Through facing difficulties, we learn to be wise.

All men, all things, have the potential to inspire. I am confident that when we have sufficient investigation into our natures that all of us will find we are compelled to the conclusion that all men are potential mediums. All men have the ability to become alert and sensitive to another power, to other sources of power both seen and unseen, whichever is ready to spring forth. It comes because an avenue has been made for it.

You see, it is the moment of crisis, the approach to the grand climax, the special occasion, that makes the heaviest demands upon this power of inspiration. Here is the scope for the unconscious to leap forth to the rescue of the conscious which is yearning for the power of inspiration. It is this moment of crisis, this special occasion which compels us to rise. This is the acid test, because the crisis demands Success with a capital S. There must be no compromise here.

Too often we fail to rise to the occasion. Why is this so? I think there are two main reasons. Firstly, there are those who fail because they make their attempts too much of a solo effort. They forget to make use of other sources of power that are there waiting for them to call upon, waiting to breathe through them.

Secondly, there are others who fail for the very opposite reasons. They pin their faith completely outside their own ability. Some believe that the mythical God of good fortune will smile kindly upon them. Others hold firmly to the belief in their priest and are content to take along to him all their cares and problems.

Others believe that lighting a particular candle, the utterance of a special prayer or sound will bring about the desired result. Let us not forget the alleged Spiritualist who is content to leave all in the safe-keeping of his medium or his guide. He is equally stupid, foolish and wrong.

The crisis can only be met when we are prepared to make all possible use of our individual efforts, to strain to the fullest extent our every nerve and talent. Then — and only then — in all humility, when we acknowledge that this individual effort (although very necessary and part of the divine plan) is, in itself, not enough, will we arrive at the moment of inspiration.

In true humility we must learn to blend ourselves with other sources of power, with other men, with other souls. Only in this way is the fuller measure of inspiration made possible.There is nothing artificial about this unless it is that in the barriers which we seem to put in the way of the power by our own ignorance of psychic law.

It is easy to appreciate that our mind, our highest consciousness, can be influenced by such things as books, poetry and music. But the moment we infer that the mind can be influenced by an unseen consciousness which is distinct and separate from the conscious self we meet with intellectual opposition. Why should this be so difficult to imagine?

As I have already said, the mind cannot be explained physically. Its very nature belongs to the law of the psychic. The psychic has the power to absorb not only the things which can be seen, heard and felt by our physical senses, but also to absorb the unspoken thought and express the feelings of other minds. The psychic nerves are the feelers of the mind darting out and thrusting forth; then absorbing, they are our powers of perception, but powers of perception which see beyond the obvious.

Experimental work into the nature of the psychic reveals that the psychic faculties are unlimited by our perception of time; that emotion or the experience of some dim and distant moment, or some moment yet awaiting birth, can become the emotion, the experience of the self in this moment called now. When this psychic faculty is allowed its true, natural flow, it is then we begin to see that it is but a hint of a greater power, a greater power even more mysterious.

But having learned to exercise our own individual power, our own individual ability, we must successfully blend with other sources of power, other souls. After that, we are justified in resigning our being to the divine order which is there ready to breathe itself through the more highly evolved souls. This is a secret which the true medium quickly learns: that beyond this consciousness-possessed intellect, there is a newer, greater energy; that beyond his private power as an individual there is a spiritual source from which he can draw.

In this way, the ethereal tides of celestial climes can circulate and flow through the medium. With an air of abandonment, he lends himself to the celestial and becomes ethereally embraced. He is caught up in the very life stream of the universe. He partakes of the true nectar of the soul, and with soul in communion with soul, all earthly barriers vanish, physical limitations are overcome, boundary walls crumble and all fetters of superstition and chains of ignorance fall away. It is this mediumistic nature of inspiration which helps us to understand so many of the problems which up until now we have been quite unable to answer.

We have been unable to answer them because we have not understood the nature of the psychic. It is not a power you can switch on or off at will. It is not a power which can be sustained for lengthy periods. What the medium can — and indeed must do — is to prepare and condition himself to be alert to its arrival. That is why I stressed the importance of preparation earlier on. It is the fluctuating nature of psychic perception that gives us fresh heart. Indeed, it is with some sense of relief that we note the great too have their faults.

What do I mean? Simply that the medium is subject to the same human weaknesses as we all are. Thus, strange though it may seem, we all the more readily respect them for the way they are, for they are after all of our own kind: flesh of our flesh. They are not superhuman, angelic, man-gods. Instead they are examples of humanity reaching out to God. Because of that very humanity, we can identify with them, relate to them, and see them as indications of our own potential.

One of the greatest mistakes made by the founders of Christianity or other saviour-god religions was to try and portray their leaders as being distinct and separate from the rest of the human race. Thus the saviour gods of other world religions bear the flavour of legend and fairy tale, and for many of us lack the seal of possibility and truth.

Before we can develop our psychic perception, we need to recognise that it exists. Once recognising its existence, we have to learn to understand it. The psychic nature of man demands the same care and attention as other aspects of his being. If you claim that the development of this psychic nature is something which can be left to chance, then I say this: when the same care and attention is given regarding the education and cultivation of man's psychic nature, as is shown to other parts of his being, then I venture to suggest that the heights reached by men will transcend our wildest hopes and our fondest dreams.

Refuse to see the psychic in terms of tea-cup reading, ghosts and fortune-telling. To limit it in this way is to say an opera singer's voice is only for grunting with. Do not shackle man's potential in this way. Do not limit it either to clairvoyance and the proof of an afterlife. That is only one function. Do not limit it to one function. The psychic is the perception of the non-physical. Every thought, every feeling, every concept and idea, all significance and meaning, is non-physical. God is non-physical. The psychic is the means of perceiving all of this.

Of course, psychic perception can never fulfil its true destiny until it is allowed to evolve and later be merged with the spiritual. The psychic grows and develops through the evolving child. How else could human beings learn to cope with ideas, feeling, sensitivity? Every time we think or sympathise we are using this psychic faculty: you can't reason with your physical senses. In fact, you can't interpret messages from those physical senses without the psychic perception playing its part. We are all psychic.

"Psychics" only appear different from average because they have learned to extend the use of this very common (this life-essential) faculty. The inspired are rare, but only because so few people understand that the faculty of perceiving beyond the physical really exists and need not be limited to perception of those who have passed, or to future events.

Once we all realise the spiritual potential of this faculty, we shall nurture it with the greatest of care, for it is our future.

Moments of inspiration are rare in history because they demand men of superior virtue, men who will stand out in the garden like flowers of super excellence. No ritual, no ceremony, is required for their ordination; similarly, no oil, holy or otherwise, is required for their anointing. The true prophet, poet or priest is ordained and anointed by the voice of the universe. Each shall be acclaimed by the verdict of history. Through them floods the power of Spirit. Through them their voices are heard, felt and obeyed by peoples of all times.

What does this say about our ideology of equality? It would seem to put it to a severe test. In the light of this understanding of inspiration, how can we claim with the poet that all men are equal? The very growth and development we have spoken of depends upon our ability to overthrow the death beetle of monotony.

If every contest between man and event was to end with the same result, if every game were to be drawn, the dull drab colour of such an order would eventually become a shroud of a world. Such a world, lifeless, would slither into the grave of its own lifelessness and indifference.

Life is an eternal variation. In the end it is this variation which shall prove the divine law based upon justice, that equality is not just the dream of the poet, not just an ideological fancy, not a meaningless catch phrase of the politician. Neither is it an empty bribe of religion. Brotherhood and the equality of brotherhood is a grim necessity.

He who is great amongst men is the true medium. The true medium is the one through whom God flows, making known the collective unconscious of the universe. It is not to the kingdom above that we need to look to see that the hand of the black becomes firmly held in the hand of the white, but here upon earth. Here and now we must realise that there are no superior colours, races or classes.

But there are superior souls. The people of every colour, race and class can become such when they are prepared to put forth a sufficiency of effort. In other words equality lies not in our present state of being, but in our potential, in our opportunity to develop that potential.

The greatest enemy of all true progress is ignorance. The philosophy of Spiritualism has succeeded in breaking through this long dark night; and in pointing its finger towards the dawn, the dawn of a newer, fairer day, the dawn which heralds the day in which man can at last become Man. It points to the day when the voice of universal life will speak through him.

His voice shall be heard by the peoples of all lands, and his message shall be heard by generations which are yet unborn. No cult or superstition shall halt or suppress him. No bars imprison, no walls confine. All pain shall cease to hurt or frustrate him. Disease will melt before his gaze, and the land and the sea and the air and all things therein shall become his. Because he breathes the breath of the living God, and lives with the full totality of his unbounded knowing and love.

Chapter Fourteen

THE DAWN OF HEALING

THE year was1941. I had worked in the mines since I left school at fourteen. It was the only kind of work available in the area. Before I started, my father talked to me man to man, and gave me virtually the only advice he ever did. He told me to work hard, and to do my very best at whatever I was asked to do. So that's what I endeavoured to do. But fourteen years on, at the age of twenty eight, I collapsed at work and had to be taken home.

The condition was serious, so serious that I heard our family doctor, Dr Ferguson, tell my father there was no hope for me. There was nothing more he could do; I only had a matter of days to live. I seemed somehow distant from the situation, as if the doctor was talking about someone else, not me. Surely it wasn't me who was going to die? But, in a sense, die I did.

The experience was beautiful. As I closed my eyes, I drifted slowly towards a bright light. Rising from my body, I breathed now in an exquisite atmosphere. It was like breathing champagne. The entire experience was so beautiful, so joyous, that I hoped never to return from it. Light was all around me. Gussie beckonned. Living became all light and freedom, a kind of rapture.

We talked wordlessly until it dawned upon my understanding that I had died. I felt no sorrow then, none, until she impressed me with the idea of "Not yet." At that she faded from my sight. A robed man came forward, an Oriental man. I later learned that his name was Yang Sang. He explained I was to be healed, gradually and slowly, and that I would live.

Yang Sang placed his hands upon me until I could feel the life force flooding through. He explained he would return to work with me regularly, but that for now, I must return to my physical body.

Oh, how reluctant I was to do that! It was so cold, dark and heavy in comparison with my new state. But return I did.

I was off work for twenty seven months in all. My convalescence was gradual but steady, earning me the title of "a bloody miracle" from Dr Ferguson. With the love and attention of doctor, family and friends, I began to live again. It was as my health began to rebuild that healing really began.

While we were still living in Tydfil Terrace, a lady came to live opposite us. I had never met Mrs Evans personally as I was still in the later stages of convalescence so was surprised when she came to the house to say she wanted me to help her. Her problem had brought her almost to her wit's end, and it was her brother who came to her aid. Very calmly, he told her that from where he stood, he could throw a stone to the house of the man who could help her. "His name is Mr Ford," he said. What made him speak that way, I shall never know, but as a result, she found herself in our house asking for help.

Without enquiring what the problem was, I asked her to give me the ring she was wearing, and held it loosely in my hand. From that I could tell she was worried, and that she had a decision to make concerning a young baby. She told me I was correct. Feeling more confident in me now, Mrs Evans explained that her husband was doing National Service, and that tomorrow, she had to go alone to the hospital and make a decision about the treatment of her baby girl who was seriously ill.

"Have no fear," I said. "You won't have to make a decision. They'll tell you to take the baby home."

The next day in hospital, the doctors told Mrs Evans to take her baby home. At four months, the child was too young to be operated on. Her mother was told that her young daughter would not live more than a week, and that she was to take her home to die.

Our neighbour was hysterical when she returned home, sobbing over and over, "There's nothing we can do!" Yet her young sister, Sharon, continued to offer her hope. "Go back to Mr Ford," she said. "He was right before. Perhaps he can help you again."

She came over to us again at 7 o'clock that evening. We arranged for her brother (who lived two doors down), my mother,

Miss Charles, John Williams, Sharon and Kate to be there too.

The hour arrived, and we sat in circle. Yang Sang (the robed figure who had helped me so greatly in my own illness) worked with us. He said that whatever was there in the child's spine would be drawn out gradually. We continued to sit regularly. As time went by, thankfully the child did not die as predicted. Instead, the growth developed on her spine.

One day it erupted. We were relieved to think that the healing process was over. It was natural to hope that the problem was overcome, but I was told that although the girl would be quite well for a few months, the growth would come again: the process could not be rushed.

She was free of it for four months. We were told that when it reappeared, we should sit regularly again for a few weeks and finish the job. This we did, and I instructed Mrs Evans to place warm Welsh flannel upon the lump. One day, Yang Sang asked her if she had seen anything on the flannel. "Yes," she said. "I saw a spot of blood." This was the sign that the work was complete.

Such is the power of Spirit that Anne, the baby, now has children of her own, and lives in Surrey from where she still drops me a line from time to time.

That was the beginning of the working relationship with Yang Sang which continues to this day. With him I have learned that although healing may be through physical contact, it can occur just as frequently through talking or listening to the patient. Healing works through love, care and sympathy, not through certificates or rote learning. It is literally the breathing of life back into the body.

Not unconnected with these experiences is the best demonstration of materialisation I ever witnessed. It was with the medium Alec Harris in Cardiff.

In the late forties, I organised a bus to take over twenty of our members to a sitting with him at his home where he worked. The room was a fairly large one, large enough to take twenty five or so people arranged in rows forming a semi-circle. In one corner was the cabinet in which Alec sat. Our members formed a semi-circle in front of it. From this cabinet, the materialised forms emerged. I was sitting next to Mrs Harris, with my head bowed, which is why

I did not at first notice what was happening.

Suddenly, one of our group recognised the form of Yang Sang. Their exclamation of excitement drew my attention to him. He came directly to me and caught my hand until I was standing beside him. He felt perfectly human and normal to my touch.

What wonderful evidence that was for us! Not only were we seeing Yang Sang after working so closely with him over the years, but we were listening too. He spoke to each one of us individually.

Now, Yang Sang had worked through me regularly for years at my home circle so members were perfectly familiar with him. One by one, he went to each, and continued in Alec Harris's room the conversations he had begun with them in my home, as if they had never been interrupted.

Yet most impressive of all was the voice that awakened my intense attention: it could only be one person who was calling. Looking up, I could see my mother's face wreathed in both smiles and tears as Gussie appeared before her. My sister, as a girl of nine, ran to her mother with arms wide. They hugged and spoke as if the intervening years had never been. Here was all the evidence of spirit return that anyone could ever ask for.

It is its own reality. It is the ultimate healer of grief.

Chapter Fifteen

SOUL PERCEPTION

HOW many bodies do you have? The obvious answer is, "One!" It is obvious because your physical body is the only one you can see. How could you possibly have any more? Well, if you think you have a body and a spirit, then you might want to claim you have two bodies: a physical body and a spiritual body.

Some books will tell you that you have almost as many as you can think, each one being a vehicle or receptacle for your soul to be carried around in, or protected by. If you can think of the soul as being the kernel of you, the real you, then perhaps a simple dictionary definition can help you to understand something about the number of bodies you might have.

You see, the soul is described as the animating part of you. It is the part of you which is emotional, moral and intellectual. In fact, it is just about everything apart from your physical body! The definition gives us a clue: apart from being physical, we are emotional, and mental and intellectual and vital beings. We are all of these things, and if you think about it, each has its own sensitivity: each has its own way of knowing about the world.

Your physical body will tell you whether the day is warm or cold. Your emotional body will tell you if it is a happy day of not. Your mental body will tell you the day of the week and what month it is while your intellectual body allows you to dwell on the passage of time and its significance. In that sense, we have a "body" or sensitivity for each kind of knowing we have.

Some older religious teachings link the physical to the non-physical bodies through what they call an etheric body, one that gradually dissipates or disintegrates after the death of the physical body. In a simplified form, their understanding is that we have five bodies: the physical, etheric, astral (or desire body), the lower mental, which masters facts, and the higher mental, which is capable of wisdom and understanding. Each is a vehicle for the soul, your individual essence-of-life. Maybe the soul is our ultimate "body." This would give us six in all.

Say for a moment then that we really do have six bodies. Does it matter? Do you need to know how many bodies you have? Millions of people have lived their lives without either knowing or caring. However, it might be interesting to consider the possibility. I'll tell you why.

If you think of a human being as only a physical entity, then you do so in terms of someone who needs food, clothing and shelter. You will not understand much of what he does, and you will not be able to help him grow to his full potential. You may feed him physically, but who is to feed him emotionally, mentally or spiritually if no one recognises that there are other aspects of him? Under such circumstances, he has to remain perforce partially undeveloped. The more facets we recognise in man, the more we can nurture and develop him.

Once man has understanding, he has the key to mastery. Part of the soul's nature is to understand. It uses its various "bodies" to draw information from experience of life. The soul can then process into its own wisdom and understanding that same experience and understanding. By perceiving life — observing it, apprehending it — the soul learns.

It therefore learns through the physical, through the emotional, through the mind and the soul itself until deep understanding is achieved. The aim of this chapter is to look at perception and how it has developed in the human being in the hope that we can identify the ultimate form of perception, the spiritual understanding I call "soul perception."

Imagine what it would be like if we were purely physical with no sensitivity: it would be dark in the world if there was no feeling. Even if the earth were lit with millions of stars and thousands of suns, though they would make visible the blue skies, rolling oceans, mountain peaks, the valleys and dells, the eyes of the new born in our world with no sensitivity, would gaze on them in vain. Not until we evolved sufficiently the ability not only to see but also to feel would we become aware of our surroundings.

Let us go further. It would be silent in the world if there was no feeling. Music's melodious symphonic strains would fall to no avail upon the ears of the unfeeling. To them the poet's voice speaking an image clothed in words would have no meaning, no matter how fine.

Deeper than all thought, then, deeper than all speech, deeper than all things which are or yet shall be, is the unnameable something which feels: deep, deep in the heart of things.

There has to be a bridge between the part of us which is physical, and the deep feeling part at the core of us. Perhaps the first touching point is what is referred to sometimes as the etheric body.

Closely linked with the physical, the etheric body is essential to physical life, but is said to disintegrate weeks after physical death. We may not understand it, but we do know it is the first mechanism of feeling, of sensitivity. Like a catalyst, this mechanism for responsiveness brings a special moment of consciousness to each of us.

From that dim and distant moment, which no finger can trace, no searching penetrating mind behold, darkness begins — perhaps but slowly, very slowly — to give place to light. Life begins not only to move and grow; life feels its movement and its growth. It becomes conscious.

Life can only feel a meaning in a day when it has also felt the evening shadows slowly gather and known the black curtains of night to fall. The darkness of night gives meaning and significance to the light of day. Our lives only become aware of sweetness and beauty when they have also been touched by the thorns which hurt and scar. In the same way, a low note is only known as such be contrast with a high note. "In" only becomes significant as "in" when "out" has been observed; long becomes long by contrast with short, sour with sweet, good with evil.

The growth and development of feeling is dependent upon contrasts. As physical life is full of contrasts, physical feeling and then emotional feeling grow and grow. Once this growth commences, there is nothing which can prevent its onward, forward march. Events may hinder, may frustrate, may misdirect, but never with finality is feeling prevented from becoming more and still more feeling.

Our universe is founded upon certain unalterable, fundamental laws; laws to which all life is subject. Let man do what he will, these laws will forever demand obedience. There is no getting away from them. One of the unalterable laws of life is that life will ever beget life. Thus feeling begets more feeling. In time, as we can predict feelings or the circumstances which lead to them, feeling begets the first glimmers of knowledge.

So we start with the unfeeling, physical material. Spirit uses this material as a tool for its own growth by building an etheric replica which when "keyed in" to the physical gives it the aspect of life. At its most rudimentary, gradually the constant flow of feeling induces responses from the physical. The physical will then feel without being conscious of that feeling. As the ability to feel evolves further, a consciousness of that feeling begins to stir. And as consciousness awakens further, knowledge is born.

Feeling, consciousness, knowing. Three of our "bodies" are involved in the process: the etheric, the astral and the mental. The sensitivity that each has gradually builds up the capacity for awareness in other bodies. Life does beget life. Response to the physical brings feeling then fuller consciousness and then knowledge.

The ultimate motive and aim of feeling is to know. With the birth of feeling the world becomes a little less dark, a little less silent. With the advent of knowledge, the hand of life stretches out more eagerly to where there is even more light and the world is even more real.

Growing, moving life becomes aware of feeling. It pauses. Life feels more strongly until it questions and wonders. Feeling grows still stronger. Still more intense becomes its deep questioning wonder. So life begins to know. Shyly it leans forward. Gaining courage, it stretches out its hand and all the while feeling grows, all the while life questions and wonders more. A little more full, a little more sure becomes the knowledge, and it begins to grasp and to hold.

"Pleasure is a shadow, wealth is variety,
and power a pageant; but knowledge is perennial in fame.
Unlimited in space and infinite in duration,

In the performance of its sacred offices it fears no danger,

Spares no expense, looks into the skies, explores sea and land,

Contemplates the distant, examines the minute,

Comprehends the great, ascends the sublime —

No place too exalted for its reach" (*De Witt Clinton*).

The first faint murmurings of knowledge becoming awake bring to us a recognition of a world of many contrasts as I mentioned before. There are even contrasts in the many effects which this knowledge has on the individual.

Knowledge can lift up his heart or fill his whole being with joy: it can subdue him or fill him with unutterable sadness. However, it affects him, he will continue to learn, for having once started on his long, long journey, the possessor of knowledge will go on and on, gathering and acquiring more and still more knowledge. There is no power on heaven or earth that can halt his growth. No power in the universe that can alter the law of knowledge's existence: the law of its being is to go on and become more and more.

Knowledge will ever beget knowledge, and as its possessor, the knower, strives to know more, he will beget or create, discover or experience ideas. Ideas or mental images point and give direction to fields of more knowledge. Often this knowledge is a long way off. Often it is a knowledge too difficult to understand, to grasp or to hold, still too vague to explain or define.

Think of it this way. Ideas are the buds rather than the blooms. Between the bud and the actual bloom of knowledge, a tremendous gulf exists. For many long and sometimes weary years, the bloom can only be imagined. The bloom is as yet unborn, unknown. But it is felt, intuited or guessed at because of the idea — the bud.

When we see a rosebud, we have faith that it will open out into a rose. We do not know that it will open, but we have faith that it will. Looking at the bud, we may also hope that when it opens it will be an exquisite bloom. So with the idea we have faith that it will develop and hope that it will develop into something profound and beautiful. The gulf between the bud and the bloom, the idea and the knowledge, man sometimes finds too long, too wide. He is reluctant to bridge the gulf, yet it must be bridged. Ideas must become more than ideas. How can this happen?

As a crystal grows silently within a solution until eventually it is visible to the observer, the idea grows within the mind until it is likened to a picture. In other words, it becomes a symbol or a mental picture. "Sinnbild" is the German world for symbol. "Sinn" means sense, and "bild" a picture so a symbol is a sense picture. This is how an idea is first expressed within the conscious mind. The symbol gives to the mind archetypes, sense-pictures or forms of truth which the intellect cannot as yet understand or grasp. Symbols are shared by many peoples, cultures and times even though their detailed interpretation of them will vary.

Because religion often deals with matters that are intuited rather than fully known and understood, the symbols of budding ideas are often found in sacred writing. They form an elemental part of the human constitution. We find them in all mythologies, fairy tales, religions, traditions, legends and mysteries. Such are always possessed of a strange magical force. They intrigue and hold us spell bound. Symbols play a tremendously important part in human growth and evolution, giving to man as seemingly nothing else can undaunted faith full of energy and life.

When they first appear in our consciousness, the first reaction is to accept them as holy or inspired in a sacred sense. Until our developing minds understand that symbols are nothing more than the visual promise of knowledge to come, we may well make the mistake of looking at its symbols as being real and true in themselves.

You can see how easy it is for confusion to reign when man worships the picture or symbol of God rather than the reality, and sees one man as God himself rather than a good example of godly qualities. The Greeks were not wrong to represent the power of God as Zeus and Aphrodite and Hercules, but they were misled when they worshipped each as a live and individual being. They mistook the symbol for reality, the bud for the bloom.

In the earlier stages of human growth, symbolism was the outcome of the instincts and feelings of the herd rather than the individual. Men lived, thought and hunted, knew only the emotions of fear, security, contentment, as a group or herd. When men saw their system of living as a herd evolve, their existence began to take the form of communal life. Instead of all doing the same task together, each was given a role to which he was best suited.

Now this had the effect of causing him to feel and to think more as a person or individual. For a long time after this change, the entire tribe would still live under the influence of the same symbols, but gradually the minds of some men would begin to outgrow their fairy tales. Slowly the symbol becomes less real, and the mind of the individual begins to discover the knowledge the symbol represents. He becomes delighted by the potential the symbol has, and from its myriad possibilities gleans knowledge he can fully grasp and make his own. The bud has bloomed. What then?

Knowledge begets knowledge. The process begins all over again, but this time from a point of greater understanding. Now the mind of the individual begins to seek new symbols, those which are more real and true. Why did Christ teach in parables, Aesop use fables or Shakespeare write poetry? Each in his own way has presented us with symbols: the Prodigal Son, the crow with the cheese, the jealous Othello, and invited us to interpret the symbols they offered. Each symbol, as potential knowledge, stimulates us to think, to reach out, to question. Each symbol teaches us what we need to know. Once the lesson is taught, that particular symbol is discarded and we await the fresh inspiration of a new picture.

The interval between the old and the new mind picture or symbol always marks the point of a great crisis in human development. History records for us that in social, political and religious life, this interval can be a most terrifying one. When individual members of a flock so grow and develop that they begin to see flaws in the symbols and teachings of their day, they face crisis. What they used to accept they now no longer find acceptable. They can (for example) no longer submit themselves to dogmatic rule. At such times there is not only confusion, but also war, bloodshed of a most fearful and terrible nature. Such is the power of the growing idea on the social scale.

A similar sequence is followed at an individual level by the developing adolescent. Much of his aggressive behaviour is in consequence of having learned from one set of symbols: mother and father as all-knowing, all-loving, all-providing. He then has to search for new ideas and symbols to "learn his way through." He turns to search for new ideas and symbols — social, political, religious, sex and status — all eagerly provided by the media, and begins his approach to adulthood by trying, tasting and sifting his way to a maturer understanding of life. Such a young individual is driven by desire: desire for experience, desire for better ideas, desire for independence, for more knowledge.

It is the feeling of revolt against the present world of ideas that brings into being desire. The quality and worth of the new idea and the new symbol is determined by the strength and intensity of desire.

"Desires are the pulse of the soul: as physicians judge by the appetite, so may you by desire," says Merton.

To want is as natural as to breathe. Wanting, however, is of itself a restless, unhappy, sad state. It is a condition which can hurt and wound. It is a state which searches for light and seeks for guidance. It was dark in the world in which we could not feel, and it is dark in the world of desire which has no sense of direction.

Where in our selves can we look for this directive force? The eyes of our minds seem set in our unconscious beings, for from the depths of our unconscious selves comes the urge to move onward and upward. At first the motive is often not known to the conscious self, but an indwelling life force, searching and struggling, prompts us ever onwards.

Beneath the layer of consciousness, there lies a layer of unconsciousness. These are not separate compartments of the human make-up. Just as the health of the physical body is determined by the natural constant flow of the blood stream, so the health of our mental self is determined by a constant, efficient flow of a psychic stream to and from our unconscious and conscious selves.

This flow generates a degree of psychic energy which in the earlier stages of life is known as instinct. Later it becomes intuition. In all stages of its development, however, its most important function has been to give a sense of direction. The continued generation of psychic energy should in time cause into being Will. Once the individual has mastered the use of will, desire should not normally remain in a negative, unhappy state for long.

136

Man is indeed a complicated being who might well be described as a world in miniature. He is a bundle of opposites, an assembly of contrasts, a being of many moods and feelings. He is both god and slave, lord and beggar. Possessed of emotions which come and go, rise and fall with bewildering rapidity, each in its turn, he is capable of atuning himself to all that this universe of worlds has to offer. If he wills it so.

But these many nerves, feelings, ideas and emotions must have a chief. There must be a "big boss," a someone to control and direct, a someone to decide. This god, occupying the throne of the human cosmos, is called the self or the ego, and the ego rules by the power of will. To want or desire is not enough — there has to be the determination to achieve. As the Chinese proverb says, "Great souls have wills: feeble ones only have wishes."

Desire then motivates the lower mind and as it develops to open the higher mind, desire becomes will. It is at this stage that a new part of man is developed. Something which has become known as personality begins to take shape and form. It is useful to remember that the words persona and personality come from the Latin word "persona" meaning mask. This is not to say that our personalities are false or deceitful, though. Just as our physical bodies need protective attire to go out into the battles of life, so our mental and spiritual bodies need a protective "cloak" to do battle with the problems, difficulties and mysteries of life.

Our personalities establish themselves through our habitual responses to life. When a response becomes "typical" of us, it becomes part of us, a characteristic which others recognise as the person we are. Personality grows and is reinforced by experience of life. We become recognised by what is different about us, by the way we contrast with the herd. We begin to stand out, so to speak, as separate.

This is known as the process of individuation, that is of becoming an individual. Previously man had been entirely subject to the instincts and laws of the herd. The laws he had known were fetish laws: the laws based upon a herd belief in the supernatural and superstitious. Under fetish law, man would worship and blindly obey what he believed were the commands of ordinary pieces of stone or wood.

The process of becoming an individual, however, has the effect — very gradually of course, but very surely — of causing man to become more and more concerned with the law of his own being. His thoughts, his feelings, his desires become more and more his own. They are separate and different from the thought, feelings and desires of others. The more personal these feelings and desires become, the stronger the will exerts itself. As a result, life is lived more intensely and seems consequently altogether more real.

You might think that developing a personality of his own and becoming an individual would mean that man becomes more removed and separate from other men, but this is not normally true. As man becomes more distinctive and separate from his fellow men, his interest is much taken up with the search for others of like mind and persuasion. Once again he becomes aware of contrasts — this time between other human beings — and in noting these contrasts, he learns more about his fellows and their variety. He approaches a deeper understanding of them. As a man becomes more himself, he becomes more other men.

Look how our awareness is focussed and deepened. The laws and life of the herd gives way to the law of life of society. That in turn grows into the law and life of brotherhoods, fellowships and friendships. Throughout this long process, man's ideas and concepts of law become less and less fetish, less and less superstitious, less and less prescriptive. Blind obedience is no longer required. What is demanded is more light, more knowledge.

When you are given just a little light, you become painfully aware of just how very dark everything else is. As a feeling, thinking, willing individual, man now has a little knowledge and is very soon aware of the vast amount that he does not know. New responsibilities, strange, frightening and wonderful, become his. His needs are now greater than ever before. The eternal prayer for more light calls forth from his being with ever increasing force. The more you have, the more you want.

To this ancient and eternal prayer, there is an eternal answer. Stealthily, quietly, mysteriously, the light of inspiration dawns in the mind of man. Spontaneously, without ceremony, unannounced, come fleeting moments of an excitingly new and wondrous power and ability. Eagerly and greedily the awakened mind leaps forth to drink its fill of this magical moment of inspiration.

What effect does this light of inspiration have? It shows up the flaws in the old and overworked symbol. It sheds its beams upon the new idea and gives birth to the new and vital symbol. For brief staccato-like moments, the mind perceives beyond the ideas, behind the symbol, and catches glimpses of the eternal truths, seeing not only the symbol, but the thing symbolised.

The pure, inspired moment permitting the mind to take succour from the fount of world consciousness, will refuse to be fettered, shackled and bound by the laws of convention and custom. Temporal science, artificial law and synthetic rationalism along with imagined logic are scorned and defied, and swept from inspiration's path. Triumphantly she strides her way through them as if they were empty, meaningless toys.

In these rare but hallowed moments, the poet in us will not be hemmed in or hampered by the verdict of science or the cold voice of logic. Undaunted, the mind will pursue its course. It knows though it cannot see. It is these brief and rare moments that first bring man to the realisation that he is a living soul.

He is not just a physical, feeling, desiring, willing, thinking being. He is a soul.

In attempting to define soul, I could be tempted to seek refuge in the famous definition of Hood:

"What is mind? No matter. What is matter? Never mind. What is soul? It is immaterial."

But perhaps Michael Angelo was nearer the mark when he wrote:

"Heaven born, the soul a heavenward course must hold;
Beyond the world she soars.
The wise man I affirm can find no rest in that which perishes,
Nor will he lend his heart to ought that doth on time depend."

So the soul is not physical, not mortal, not restricted by time. Let us say then that it is spiritual, immortal and timeless. Where does that take us? In a very simple way, it takes us beyond restrictions: the soul is free from size, shape, weight and location. It lives. It neither was nor will be: it simply is.

Can we define how it lives or what it is like? The answer is,

"Only as far as we have experienced it." How can you define your astral body or say how it lives unless you have first felt deeply and desired? How can you define your mental body if you have never thought or imagined or been conscious? Whatever understanding we may have of thought and feeling is compared and contrasted with the experience of others.

You will remember how, earlier on, I suggested these "bodies" of ours were nothing other than sensitivities or ways of perceiving. To understand each body, we need to look at our experience of its particular perception.

What then do we know of soul perception? Ordinary men and mystics alike can tell you that it is the feeling of being part of a much larger world which is the point when the soul first brings to the emotions of man the feeling that his ultimate destiny is higher than earth or clay.

Soul perception brings with it the feeling of relationship with a divine plan. Through the perception of the soul, man becomes aware with movement slow, with halting, faltering steps, of his spiritual self. Then he becomes aware of spiritual law which declares that he is significantly part of all divine creation.

To feel, to know and see not merely with his emotional, mental and physical self, but with his soul — his whole being — is soul perception. To feel and see beyond the normal range of his knowledge, to feel and see beyond the moment past, beyond the moment now, into the moment which makes time which was, and time which is, into an abiding and eternal now, this is to feel and see clearly. It is the perception of the soul.

The function of opposites and contrasts is to make life whole, complete and one. That is why we can lean so much from them. The whole is perceived in the part, whilst in the whole each part and unit is discerned.

We look down upon the quiet waters and in the gentle ripples can perceive mountains of tempestuous waves. We are caught up on the full current of life's storms and face the full blast of their rage and fury. Yet when we perceive with the soul, then at the height of the storm, we perceive the hushed stillness of infinite calm and peace. It is the perception of the only true brotherhood. I shall never be completely I without you. You, yourself, shall never become complete without becoming me. The saint and the sinner are perceived to be one and the same.

Together as the herd we perceived the symbol in order that later, as individuals, we might perceive more clearly the higher symbol — only that still later as a fellowship we might behold a symbol yet more high and great. We must become part of that fellowship so that (in giving, comparing, loving and understanding) we may become more completely ourselves. On becoming more completely ourselves we shall be merged into a still higher fellowship.

This is the outcome of all our constant gathering of knowledge; knowledge considered not as a means to an end in itself, but as a means of reaching out and understanding all forms of life, to become one with this life, to perceive life as a whole.

Entering a higher fellowship is also the outcome of the desire arising from feeling. The desire is given direction as the result of a healthy, harmonious relationship between the sub-conscious and the conscious selves, a true working relationship which gives power to the hand of will.

Preparation for the development of soul perception paves the way for the higher inspiration, permitting the ego to become sensitive to the thoughts, feelings and promptings of the profounder depths of our subconscious beings, permitting the soul to become awake and alive to the thoughts and feelings of other souls, be they souls carnate or discarnate. It permits the perception of spiritual law and brings down to their true, temporal, makeshift value the laws and verdicts of our earthly systems and worldly sciences. It gives us a new and refreshing sense of perspective.

Ageless and slave no more to time, prisoner no longer to space, the soul sees its physical body as a temporal, passing symbol for immortal desire, constant search and eternal feeling which ever shall demand higher and loftier vehicles of expression.

When an individual is able to perceive with his soul, he becomes a finer and wiser being. The more individuals there are in the world able to perceive with their souls, the more advanced and peaceful and loving the world must become. For the world is merely the sum of the individuals who inhabit it. How then can we encourage the world to advance?

Chapter Sixteen

SPIRITUAL ECONOMICS

THE study of economics is the study of the best use of scarce resources to achieve a desired aim. Our aim is to improve the world — and our resources are not as scarce as we might think. We need only use our resources more effectively than we do at present. The first step is to recognise that the resources are, in fact, there and that the aim of developing soul perception is both positive and practical. Let us start with the basics.

If man has to learn the economics of the soul, he could do worse than look at established economics of the body. The three constituents of a sound economy are:

A sound and healthy deposit or reserve account; an honest and equal sharing of effort by all the individual members involved; a plan which is flexible.

In spiritual economics (so to speak) the subconscious is the deposit. All thoughts, desires and feelings when not in use, do not cease to be: they are merely transferred to the subconscious. The health of the deposit account is determined by the health and purity of the thoughts, feelings and desires we transfer to our subconscious selves.

That is why it is so important that you choose what you read, what you watch on TV, what you take in from your friends and your environment, what your thoughts dwell on. It may well be useful to remind ourselves after a moan or a horror movie, that that is what we are "depositing" to use later as a resource.

We have suffered too much since the Industrial Revolution from the exploitation of one section of society by another. Masters have exploited workers and built up vast fortunes at the expense of widespread poverty. Workers have sought to dictate to employers at the expense of a growing mutual distrust and perhaps the exploitation of the consumers. Consumers, producers and managers all have their roles to play, but there has to be honesty and equality amongst all three parties if mutual advancement is to be attained. It can never be fully and happily attained in an atmosphere of distrust, suspicion and half truths.

We are creatures of many and varied moods, creatures of widely differing emotions. We are beings of many talents, but each of us is a member of one body, and all members must be given their true and natural place and part to play.

For our spiritual natures to grow, we must be given love and encouragement. It is the right of each to be given time and understanding. It is the right of each to be given equally the education which will help him to realise himself. "Know Thyself" commanded the teachers of old.

A sound spiritual economy demands that we make the best of our only resource: our self. Once we know even a little of our hopes and potential, we must claim the opportunity to express that self in love and service to our community. We have to involve and be involved in living to the full extent of our potential. Each day the discovered talents of our being should find their playground becoming larger, their workshop day by day becoming bigger, their field of labour increasing.

This should not be the story for one man, one group. It ought to be the story of each man, all men. Only then through mutual giving and sharing can the resource of spirit — the life within us — be put to use.

Why must the plan of our spiritual economy be flexible and not static? Because our "resource" of spirit lives: it changes all the time. It is never static. For this reason we cannot ever say the only way to spiritual development is through prayer, dance, fast or meditation. As the spirit moves and changes in an infinity of ways, so its own particular path of unfoldment will vary and change, reflecting its very nature.

If a static plan for one-ness with God were imposed, some souls would flourish, but others would be crushed by the very restrictions that served others as a strength. For sound spiritual economics, we need that flexibility. We also require a savings scheme.

We need to build up love and wisdom within us. To do that we must live our beliefs and put our wisdom into practice. Life is both our teacher and our classroom. Life is also our textbook. With every experience we are given the opportunity to respond with love or hate; with every experience we are challenged to look on with serenity or anxiety. With every person, object and event we may look upon each either positively or negatively.

The more we are positive, serene and loving, the more we deposit love and wisdom in our account. The more negative, anxious and hating we are, the more we risk spiritual bankruptcy. How we save and how much we save is completely up to ourselves.

Poor spiritual economics means that the soul or overself, when attempting to make a withdrawal from the deposit account of the subconscious, finds a condition of bankruptcy. This is why so many fail to rise to the special occasion, why in times of stress there is panic, why for no apparent reason there is a complete breakdown in the well-ordered, normal running of our conscious selves. It is the cause of neurosis; the real reason for warped and unbalanced lives. Unsound spiritual economics affect not only the individual, but as a cancerous growth, gnaws at the health of human society.

On the other hand, a sound, healthy economy has the effect of fanning the flame of higher desire, and when that happens, desire begins to fulfil its highest destiny:

It grows from the instincts of the physical.

It gives edge to all physical appetites.

It brings into awareness our emotional systems.

It coaxes the intellect and draws it into action.

On and on grow these desires until man is desiring with his whole being, wanting with his whole physical, nervous, emotional and mental self. This wholeness of wanting is spiritual desire. It is man wanting with his soul. It is also the result of a healthy spiritual economy.

The best spiritual economy attempts (in this sense) to promote spiritual hunger. In becoming aware of a spiritual hunger, man makes the attempt to feed his soul. While various organised religions endeavour to assuage this hunger, they are by no means the only ways to do so. Contrary to the opinions of many, organised

144

religions are not necessarily the most successful means of spiritual fulfilment and alas, in far too many instances, fail miserably and hopelessly in their task of giving the required food to the many souls who hunger deeply for it.

The reason for this failure to fulfil is possibly because established religions have adopted methods similar to industrial production systems. Mass produced prayers and dogmatic systems of worship, fixed symbols which do not alter or grow, static conventions and immobile customs tend in time to lose their fire and warmth, and make their formulae seem too artificial and unnatural a food for the ever-changing and evolving soul of man. Any programme of feeding the soul has to be flexible if it is to be effective.

Be it religion, or the arts or science, politics or philosophy, the soul will seek its food. The hymn writer's invitation to "Come and worship" might well have read, "Come and be nourished". The inner spiritual being of man will ever feast upon the beauty, poetry, art and love in life. Why? Because each is an expression of the harmony and perfection of the God force. Each is a product of its own time, a symbol of God expressed in terms the hungry soul of contemporary man can understand and be nourished by.

The hungry soul transmutes such symbols into spiritual experience of its own. As a result of thus feasting itself, it becomes lifted up, possessed of spiritual energy and power. This is the strength and power which enables man to perceive with his whole being: his soul.

What can we say about this perceiving, knowing, feeling, living soul? To what purpose does it wend its way through the green, green valleys and the grim, dark vales? To what end does man find himself passing through this world of many prayers and much blasphemy? A world so full of life, yet overladen with corpses. What relation has the soul of man to the eternal mysteries of the cosmos?

To feel the full, entire breath of the greatness and complete majesty of life, to be able not only to feel or see the law, but to become the law not only to feel or see life but to become life — that is the destiny of the clear-perceiving soul. With our emotions our response is subjective. With our intellect we can respond objectively.

With our souls, we are. We empathise so completely with our subject that we become it.

But our all-consuming interest will not be restricted to place or time. Engrossed, we become past, present and potential of what our soul perceives. No man is evil or a failure when we perceive him wholly this way. We sense the God in him, the hint of talent and loving to come. There is hope in all of us.

To take hold of pain and disease, to take hold of the time-worn creed, the false idea and ancient symbol, and to blend them successfully with true abiding joy and the natural vigour of health: that becomes the function of the higher will, the will of the god-like soul who perceives.

Steadfastly refusing to be cast down, stubbornly declining to be removed from any fact or made separate from any law, the soul cannot look upon death without seeing life. It sees life to be no empty bubble, no idle, meaningless, passing dream, but a very solemn, grim yet wonderful reality.

To look upon the world and see an entire nest of worlds, to see and feel the love of life: this is the only true weapon of the soul — its only power, its only force with which to meet and combat the trials and hurts of this world.

Let there be love. Soul perception is love. It loves what it sees. It sees its object lovingly. It only can be love because its source is love: the Divine who in the fulness of time blends all things into itself. Understand soul perception, and you can — you must — permit your perceiving soul to take hold of withered hopes and faded dreams, to take hold of the ideas now perished, to take hold of society with its scarred and battered systems, to take hold of worn and lifeless religion, and breathe into each the living breath of God.

Chapter Seventeen

GETTING ESTABLISHED

BY 1944, I was fit for sedentary work. "What's that?" asked the clerk at the employment exchange. "What you are doing!" I replied. I don't think he knew whether to take offence at the remark or not.

However, there was the chance of some work inspecting aircraft gear box components. The only problem was that I had to be able to read drawings and work with a micrometer. Determinedly I said I could do both, although I hadn't a clue about either, I was so desperate to be working again. I was told to be at the factory on Monday morning for a skills assessment. That meant I had to learn all there was to know about both over the weekend.

By her first marriage, Kate had a daughter, Mary, and a son, Owen. I knew Owen well and taught him to play an instrument in the band. Before my illness had affected my lungs, I had played tenor horn with them. Now it was my turn to ask a favour. Owen was an apprentice at the time, and knew about both diagrams and micrometers. This time he taught me. I suspect we made a good teacher and pupil, for on the Monday morning I convinced my potential employers that I was a capable worker, and got the job.

Unfortunately, the job was mine only until the end of the war, so within the year I was on the lookout for employment again.

Every day for the two years of my illness, Kate had visited me, never missing a day. We married in 1945. Our "honeymoon" was an afternoon at the pictures in Cardiff! Then we returned to our new life together in Park Place, on the other side of the valley from my parents' home.

We had two daughters, Elizabeth and Ann. Elizabeth died at

four months, but I'm very glad to say Ann is alive and well, married to John, and mother of my grandson David.

My next job was part-time sales with a toy manufacturer. I enjoyed this, travelling with my employer and persuading reluctant shopkeepers to buy, but as a married man, I could not earn sufficient to keep a household. I abandoned sales in favour of work with a hardware retailer.

This developed into full-time work in his polish factory as manager. The pay was still meagre, especially once Kate and I had our daughter Ann, but the job did have one advantage: the company owned the old St David's Church in Wyndham Street in Troedyrhiw and used it as a warehouse. They decided to sell it, and I, without so much as permission or money from my Spiritualist church, bought it on the spot, knowing that somehow we would get the required amount of money together. We did, and are still proudly in our refurbished premises forty five years on!

In 1950 for the Festival of Britain, and again in 1951 for the Festival of Arts, I was invited to sit on the Council of Ministers. This was a group of local ministers who came together to organise the religious side of the celebrations and activities. It was good that at last Spiritualism could be treated on equal footing with orthodox religion. We are brothers, not adversaries. Each should be offering his own kind of help to those who wish to understand themselves and God more fully. Between us, we organised services. I gladly took part in Church of England services, and the co-operation between us promoted greater involvement and interest in what each had to offer.

I think, as I look back, that one of the things I am most proud about is bringing an air of respectability to Spiritualism where I live. In the early days, Spiritualists by and large were outcasts (and in some cases, justifiably so) but as time passed in Troedyrhiw, I was invited on occasions to speak in their churches and share services with them. That has been a worthwhile achievement.

Chapter Eighteen

THE HUMAN MACHINE.

MAN, who can grapple with the riddles of the universe, and wrench from the earth and the heavens so many of creation's closely guarded secrets, remains confounded when confronted with the mystery of his own self.

There have been many attempts to bridge the gap between the knowledge and mystery of man. Efforts have been made by science, by philosophy and by religion, but each has failed to bridge this gap mainly because it has fallen into the mistake of thinking that the material and the spiritual are two distinct and separate states of being. This idea is wrong.

Many who would follow a spiritual path have attempted to explain away materialistic doctrines, but they inevitably fail. They fail because common sense is affronted by their arguments. Anyone can see that matter is, that it exists. No one can convincingly advance the case for spiritual awareness by ignoring this material reality.

Spiritualism, as I understand it, differs from these dismissive approaches because its adherents do not attempt to cast out or to explain away the ideas of their opposite numbers, the materialists. Instead, it is the function of the reasoning Spiritualist to breathe into the materialists' ideas a freshness which flows from Spiritualism's fuller knowledge and understanding. With such an understanding, man should face fewer crises of confidence because he will know how he works and what his nature is.

In this way, it has been hoped by more astute and enlightened minds of our age that the philosophy of Modern Spiritualism might provide the knowledge mankind requires, the knowledge which

149

will provide the bridge to link the material and spiritual together with a deeper sense of reality.

One of the most popular ways of explaining the nature of man is to liken him to a machine. Such a theory (put simply) says that you do what you do because you must. It is the theory of mechanical, impulsive action and blind instinctive behaviour. It suggests that the universe is a vast and complex motor which generates all activity and energy, and that you advance or retreat by its force. By its force you smile or weep, curse or praise, because there is no alternative. You are a small cog in a big machine.

Whether you feel inclined to accept the theory or not, you may be surprised to find how widespread and popular it is. It is easy to visualise, and easy to understand. It states that man is merely a processor of his environment. There is a comforting sense of dependable regularity in this effortless approach to the unfoldment of nature and action in man.

Flick the switch, press the button or strike the match, and you will obtain the given result. You feel in control, certain. The switch of thought or word, button of vision or sound, the match of environment: when flicked, pressed or struck, will cause to emerge forth the predictable result — Man the soldier, Man the priest, Man the poet or Man the lover.

It was Plato who first tried to make use of this mechanical theory to draw a blueprint of a planned and well-organised, happy society where, by correct use of breeding, environment, education and culture, we could have the dependable mechanical man. He thought we could construct a society of order, achievement and peace. By his method we were to have men without passions and affections, who were neither to laugh nor to weep, to feel sorrow nor anger, to be cast down nor elated by anything.

This was a blueprint which could never exist, except in the mind of its inventor. The mechanical conception is of itself incomplete. What is lacking? He left out the spiritual essence of man, the essence which shall of itself outlast Plato's philosophic Republic.

It is obvious to anyone who feels or cares that man is more than a machine. A machine is inert. It is a physical object powered by energy outside itself. It has no consciousness, no volition and

150

no control of the process. It has no sensory perception, no emotion, no aspiration, no inspiration. It cannot reproduce itself, but it can be exactly replicated.

His physical body is a life system. If, like a plant or any other animal, he is given the correct environment, feeding and care, he may develop into a fine physical example of the species. In this way he can be manipulated. Similarly, if his mind is educated and trained, and his life experiences carefully selected, he may develop into a fine intellectual example of the species. I say "may" because his development is dependent upon the will of the individual to a greater or lesser extent. It is because of his power of will or volition that man can never be entirely predictable. Therefore he can never be entirely controllable. If he is a machine, he is not a dependable one.

Even so, I have called him a human machine. Despite all the obvious arguments I have presented you with, I still offer you this notion to consider. Before you reject it, think for a moment of what a machine is. One definition is: an instrument directing application of force. Another is: an organised system for carrying out specific functions.

I agree with the materialists that the human being is a physical entity which exists, and that its physical existence is significant. I agree that the human body has specific functions which are highly significant, and cannot be ignored. But I go beyond these. Any anatomist or physiologist will tell you what the functions of the body are, and I would simply add that there are more functions than these.

Once these extra functions have been identified, you may begin to understand my claim that the human being is a machine. It is an instrument for the application of spirit to physical life; and it is an organised system for carrying out the development of soul.

The human body is a machine. The human spirit is the user of that machine. The spirit uses the machine to make the spirit grow.

Here is a table which draws together the ideas I want to get over. I am assuming here that your spirit "starts" at conception as a spark of life generated between the positive force carried by the sperm, and the negative carried by the ovum.

PHYSICAL	SPIRITUAL 1	SPIRITUAL 2
embryo	"spark" of spirit	–
body	etheric body	–
feeling/emotion	mediumship	–
consciousness	soul perception	–
thought/intellect	inspiration	mental body
independence	individuation	spiritual body

So, with the fertilisation of the ovum, the earliest spark of spirit is generated. Your soul has begun, if you like. Let us stay with the physical being for a few moments.

Look down the list under the "Physical" heading. You see the kind of progress I have mentioned in earlier chapters. The embryo develops gradually into the body which in turn begins to feel and have emotions. Consciousness develops there. Through and beyond birth, body, feeling and consciousness continue to develop, as do thought and the intellect.

Day and daily, the infant learns independence, but even well into adulthood, we are still striving to stand freely on our own two feet. This list of developments is not strictly sequential. Each development will continue to deepen and widen throughout life's experience.

It is not a matter of emotions growing until they achieve maturity before consciousness starts, and consciousness ceasing to develop as the intellect flourishes. Each of these functions weaves its way in and out of the growth of the others, changing as it goes.

Now, as the embryo makes a home for that first spiritual spark, so other stages in the physical and mental development of the human being generate something significant in the spiritual order of things.

Let's look now at the heading "Spiritual 1." The etheric body is the finer, energy field of the physical body. Whatever your physical size and shape, there is an etheric counterpart to it. Animals and plants (all things that live) have such an etheric body. It is sometimes called the subtle body because it is finer or less dense than the physical, and can be seen by mediums and psychics.

This non-physical body is generated by the living physical

152

body, and reflects the state and health of that physical body. I suggest the generation of the etheric body is one of the functions of the physical body. It is a product of the human machine.

As the physical body is still developing in the womb, it begins to feel, and to experience emotion. Later this feeling will develop further into the knowing we call instinctive or intuitive. It first learns to love in its mother's arms, in family life and through friendships. Loving and knowing are the prime functions of the spirit. Both begin in feeling.

As this ability to feel grows, so does the potential for mediumship. An essential of mediumship is the ability to feel and to empathise. As our capacity to feel grows, so does its spiritual counterpart, the astral body. It is sometimes referred to as the desire body, and after the death of the physical, will become our new vehicle of experience.

Consciousness evolves throughout our lives when it is encouraged to do so. It blends in with the development of intuition on the one hand, and the power to think on the other. Good parents endlessly talk to and entertain their offspring. Each thing they do encourages the growing young mind to become more aware of its surroundings, and more interested in them. Every experience in life becomes a similar invitation to the developed mind.

Consciousness or awareness may not always be the focussed knowing of the rational mind. It might be more vague, more emotional, freer from doubt. It is an all-embracing approach to life which seeks to understand the whole as opposed to the part. Consciousness is encouraged by the five physical senses, but its unfoldment is exciting because it bridges the gap between the physical and the spiritual, until man's awareness of the physical and the spiritual can be equally acute.

This time the mental development's spiritual counterpart is what I call soul perception. And just as the embryo awakes to consciousness in its mother's womb, so the embryo soul awakes to consciousness of the spiritual world in the womb of earth life. The purpose of this is of course, to prepare the soul for its second birth (or physical death) into the world of spirit.

So the human machine (the physical body) has generated the etheric body, the astral body, soul perception. Just as I use the machine of a car to move me from place to place, so I use the machine of my body to move me from one phase of spiritual development to another.

We send our children to school so that they may learn to think, to puzzle out problems and work things out for themselves. They need this skill of thought because it will help them to survive in difficult situations, and life is (after all) very often a difficult situation! Some people consider thinking as little more than the function of memory, but the mature thinker uses thought as a creative tool which will suggest options, evaluate and make informed decisions. He will also use it to understand others and their ideas as fully as possible. The more he exercises his mind (be it on physical or spiritual things does not matter) the more of a mental body man builds for himself in spiritual terms. His physical body is gradually equipping him for life in the spirit world.

Now, whereas the development of consciousness forms the bridge between this world and the next, the development of the power of thought widens that bridge until it can carry two-way traffic.

What do I mean by this? I mean that if a man has highly developed awareness and a capacity for thought, then he can receive inspiration: ideas from those who have grown wiser than he, who wish to act as spiritual teachers to him. He need not be aware of their influence specifically, but the ideas will come to him all the same. He will only receive what he is capable of understanding, which is why he needs to train himself in thought if he wishes the inspiration to be worthwhile. However, his mental development on earth will have allowed the development of the faculty of inspiration: a spiritual faculty.

Once the toddler has learned to walk, he learns to walk away from his parents, although he will soon tumble back again. Once he has learned to choose, he will soon choose for himself. When an adolescent learns to earn money, he will generally learn to be independent of his parents. In other words, as we learn, we apply our learning to become more independent. This is not to say that we wish to be free from all other people and influences — far from it — but until we are independent, we cannot give fully of ourselves because our selves do not belong fully to us.

Jung looks at this process and describes it as "individuation." He suggests that many adults do not achieve this by the end of their physical lives, but then the process is a psychic one, and the physical life is simply where it starts off. Achieving this state of wholeness, this integration of all aspects of the psyche, marks the attainment of soul maturity. It may happen in this life, or the next, but it has been promoted by the experience of physical life.

Our physical bodies are the midwives of our spirits, they are the machines which process spirit into souls. As such, each delicate machine requires the very best attention we can give it. It has to be loved and tended as carefully as any plant, pet or prize species. Why? Because the product will depend on the fineness of the human machine.

Neither must we lose the Users' Manual or the instruction booklet. We must not lose them, because it is all to easy to forget that our bodies are not us, but only the machines we use. Imagine for a moment a ballet dancer, one of the best in the world. Imagine that he drives his car into the open spaces of the countryside. He is so overcome by the beauty of the landscape that he wants to dance for the pure joy of it all. Imagine his frustration and misery when, locked in the car, he finds the car won't leap with him.

The example seems ridiculous. Fancy a dancer thinking that his car could dance with him locked inside it! Well, fancy a spirit thinking that his body could soar to the highest heights with him locked inside it! Our bodies are machines like cars are machines. They are useful as far as they go, but they only go so far.

If we remember that, we shall not find ourselves faced with quite so many frustrations and disappointments in life. Our bodies are there to help us to grow. But just as the dancer will open the car door and get out, so one day, we too shall step out and be free of the machine which was once of so much use to us.

In the meantime, we must learn to remember that we (our spirits) are in control of the human machine, not the other way round. It is all too easy today to consider that you are the machine. You work to regular hours; you are expected to produce a certain amount of work; you are paid for the product; you are expected to spend the payment on your predictably sized family, house, car, holiday, entertainment, etc, etc.

You seem to be a machine programmed to produce and then to consume. It takes a little while to hold back sometimes and remember that first and foremost this human machine was designed for the use of the human spirit which is by nature free.

Inherent in all men is the urge to be identified with the society of their time. Mechanically, man will go to any length just to prove that he is a man of "his place," of "his time," of "his kind."

Montaigne said, "It is the rule of rules and the general laws of laws, that every person should observe the fashions of the place where he is."

Here, more than anywhere else, we find man unreasonable in his reasoning because he is unconscious of (or has forgotten) the freedom of his spirit which was intended to use the machine. Without depth of thought or feeling, without strength of purpose, he steps in line.

In order to be fashionable and up to date, he moves forward with mock earnestness and synthetic sincerity. In the name of fashion he will adorn himself in the garb of absurdity and sham. He will exhaust himself in a desperate endeavour to follow the trend, grind himself into dust so that the God of Custom will be obeyed.

This is man the machine — or rather the man whose machine has run away with him. This is man, the slave to conformity, the prisoner chained to the demands of tradition, fashion, environment or circumstance. Is the trend war? Man must conform. Is it enterprise, self-satisfaction, nostalgia? Man must fill the bill.

Of course, conformity need not always be negative or destructive. It has to be admitted that fashion can improve as well as corrupt. In the name of fashion and conformity, we can have our ideas and put on our masks of healthy living or piety and join in this version of pretence, making it seem that we enjoy being virtuous.

But this is all part of the great bluff or illusion of life. We need to make people more aware that such a mechanical order is shallow, and empty, and sham. Then man will slowly see that in his eagerness to identify himself with the mob or the mass or today, he makes himself a non-entity and thus defeats the whole purpose of the "human machine" which is to develop the spirit of each into an individual soul.

The point where he understands that he is in charge of the

machine that can serve him: that is his real moment of birth. For then new and strange longings will awake and become alive in him. He will look out with eyes which not only see, but also perceive. His being will be filled with a soul which feels with a consciousness which knows.

With the birth of this new degree of awareness, man becomes conscious of a responsibility: not to the herd, the mob or the mass, but to himself. This consciousness of personal responsibility brings with it a new conception of reality. The new conception emerges, flowing direct from its true and natural source. This natural source is his spirit within...the user of the machine.

Only from within can we begin to understand something of the great riddle of life. Paradoxically, brotherhood is really achieved not by trying to be like other men, but by asserting our own individuality and defending the right of others to their own. The best contribution that any man can give to society is himself. And to become himself.

To become himself, man must show that he is something more than a mechanical repetition of custom and tradition, more than an inspired imitation of other men. Eventually, it is back to this power that springs from within that each of us must turn. The power of the earth or of the heavens can never be ours to grasp or hold until we allow the user of the human machine to take on its rightful position of command. Then the power of our own spiritual self will emerge.

As this applies to each individual in his own life, so it applies to Spiritualists who would have Spiritualism function to its best effect. Our growing spirits can learn to make the most of earthly experience. They can also learn to make the most of the knowledge which has been handed down to them as Spiritualism. Only when feeling, consciousness and thought have constructed the two-way bridge between the spirit world and this one can we make full use of this knowledge.

The spirit of each man, then, uses the human machine to develop his own spiritual growth. As he uses his machine more effectively and sensitively, he realises that he is a medium who can absorb and be absorbed by Divinity. He can embrace and be embraced by a power which springs from the very source of life.

This power, through man the medium, strives always to breathe a spirit of life and motion into the universe and into man himself.

Chapter Nineteen

THE PROCESS OF MEDIUMSHIP

MEDIUMSHIP is a basic and very necessary part of the human make-up. The only difference between men is that in some the gift is more developed than in others. It is latent in all. Indeed it is one of the most important and fundamental principles of life. Mediumship is an essential part of life's process.

To understand this fully, we should dispel the idea that mediumship is solely concerned with proving spirit survival after death. Mediumship is the reaching out of mind beyond what we already know, feel or understand.

Doctors, teachers, scientists, philosophers, poets, musicians and men of all strata of society, from all walks of life, of all colours and of all kinds, are moved forward by the compelling urge of this power. Moved by the mediumistic impulse, man boldly becomes more inventive. Adventurously, he looks for new heights to conquer. Bravely he seeks to explore paths hitherto untrod.

Consider the phenomena of art and genius. I claim that genius is mediumship and that art is a skill. Enter into the field of poetry, music, science or engineering, or indeed any other field of activity or work that you care to think of, and the first requirement is to master the art of that work. You are required to learn the mechanical process or techniques of your vocation or trade. For most people, mastery of the art or acquisition of the skill is enough. It is enough because it is all that is required of them to make a living. In this sense, they are quite happy to become slaves to the popular demand of their day. The reward of the material is a greater inducement to them than the realisation of a higher taste or culture.

With the genius, however, we have someone who seems

159

almost entirely to disregard the mercenary value of his work. He is equally dismissive of popular opinion, flattery or applause. To work is sufficient reward for him. He exhausts the totality of his being in unlimited indulgence of effort. Unsparingly, he grapples with impossibilities in a desperate endeavour to deliver from his soul some fragments of his greater self.

Like attracts like. This means that if a man endeavours with his whole soul to be creative in his thinking and production, he will become a constant invitation to the inspiration of higher beings. Mind blends with mind. The faint trickle becomes a stream; the flickering glimmer becomes a flood of light which illuminates the way for men as yet unborn.

Spiritualism fulfils its most valuable function when it explains to man that each man has the genius of his own developing spirit to bring to its full potential. It explains, when ears will listen, that the restrictions of the body are not the restrictions of the soul. We each have the potential for great joy in life, yet too often we let that slip away because we believe we are little more than mechanical.

Whenever we speculate upon the realms of higher awareness which other people's genius hints at, and we see hopes of being able to break free from the captivity of the fixed mechanical order, something always seems to break down. We are just at the point of touching something which is at least on the borders of the spiritual when a difficulty arises. That hint of what could be remains all too often a promise unfulfilled. The hope of it fades before we have cause to hope enough. The taste of our melted dreams is all too faint and too brief. And all because we believe the human machine is in command of us, rather than the other way round.

Look what happens. The great leader emerges. A man of genius treads our earth. The golden voiced poet speaks to us in the language of the Gods. A musician arrives and fills the air with sounds that seem to flow direct from heaven. In each case our earth is graced by souls garbed in greatness, so alert, alive and sensitive that it seems that even the freshness of the morning dew might scorch or blister them.

Wonderful! But the moment passes and they are gone. Once more we find ourselves in the rut of mediocrity, back in the cold and shallow groove of mechanical reaction. We have become ordinary and mundane once more now that our flight of fancy is over. Why cannot we maintain such a heightened spiritual state? Because we have forgotten the two-way bridge that our consciousness wrought for us, because we have forgotten the mediumship which allows each one of us to attain our own inspiration, our own genius and because we believe mechanically that great thoughts, great upliftment, is for others and not for us.

A bird only stays aloft through the power of its own wings. We have forgotten how to fly.

Genius, and in this sense, mediumship, cannot be taught: it must spring from within. To aim for such genius may encourage cleverness and talent, but never greatness. Why? Because the basic requirement of both greatness and good mediumship is goodness. And goodness can only grow in the soil of humility.

Quite clearly, there is a difference between the term "medium" as understood by the Spiritualist and "medium" in the broader and more general sense in which I have just been speaking. However, as I have already stated, it is to Spiritualism that many people do turn in order successfully to bridge this difference of interpretation.

The case for Spiritualism rests upon the particular forms of mediumship which were developed and cultivated with the express purpose of providing communion between the people of our earth and the spirit world.

The first object of that communion is very naturally to provide a measure of comfort to the bereaved, and secondly to give to the student and investigator evidence of the continuity of life. This measure of comfort and evidence is the direct result of communication from the world of spirit, which comes to us by means of mediumship.

But important though these objects are, there is a natural sequence which should develop from this form of communion. If spirit intelligences are capable of providing knowledge to give us comfort and evidence regarding the continuity of life, then they must also be capable of sharing with us the benefit of their broader and fuller experience. And it is just here that it seems Spiritualism falls short of its early promise or, to be more correct, it is just here that Spiritualists fail Spiritualism, for although the faculty of imagination is their greatest gift, it can also be their greatest drawback.

Imagination may manifest itself through fiction. Now fiction is quite honest in its dishonesty. It is an open and deliberate attempt to manufacture an idea or series of ideas, and then to translate them into any of the arts. This has become a very desirable and necessary part of our culture. It performs the most valuable functions of entertainment, amusement, education and even inspiration.

However, we must also look at imagination in what I choose to call its purest form. This is when it is fired or stimulated into being by what philosophers call the "true idea." This time imagination becomes the very life blood of creative life. It is induced into being by experience of any impulse, desire, emotion or sensation. Indeed it would be true to say that imagination seizes upon any given thing and claims it as its own raw material to form as it will. Anything and everything becomes the wings of imagination as it soars heavenward and from heaven to earth returns once more.

It takes hold of nothingness and moulds it into the habitation of reality. Under its inspired gaze, the tree it transforms into the boat, the house, the temple. Its touch of divinity transforms the plot of waste land and a few stones into a city.

In hesitant but majestic step, thought leaps forth unto thought, and from that sacred wedlock is born all that which proclaims in unerring certainty all the glory and beauty, the elegance and grace, all the radiant brilliance of a universe that is ours to grasp and hold.

Imagination in this form has a full part to play in the development of psychic awareness. Imaginative psychic feelers dart out into the path ahead. They delve and probe into realms unknown, and fulfil an invaluable function in all forms of communion with the spirit world.

But imagination also manifests as illusion. This flows directly from what we call the "false idea." The "true idea" of the philosopher is the substance of creative life; the "false idea" is the disease which pollutes all pure and natural expressions of life. The true idea through imagination unveils the process of natural law, leads us along the pathway to truth, inspires, coaxes and entreats the mind to new effort and achievement. It bathes the soul in its waters of reality and revelation.

Illusion is the counterfeit of all that is true and natural. It is the great bluff, the weapon of the cheat and the fraud. It is the breeding ground of neurosis, fear and deceit. The medium who falls victim of illusion becomes the arch enemy of Spiritualism. Indeed, illusion by sinister stealth distorts and corrupts at every level.

How do you know the difference between the true idea and the false one? There is no easy answer, but perhaps Christ's reply of "By their fruits shall ye know them" is the best we can find. We can only look at the effect of our thoughts and ideas, and deal with them accordingly.

Spiritualists know of the remarkable potential that is man's. They know the power of imagination, the power of thought, the power of mediumship, yet like everyone else, they limit themselves.

Henry Ford said, "Whether you think you can, or whether you think you can't, you're right."

Always it seems that Spiritualists are content to preach of the good which could be done. There is always a qualification there. They need to enable it to be done, for there is the world of spirit with a wealth of knowledge and experience which could benefit the whole of our society if we would only use it, if we would only put it into operation. The vastness of this limitless source of matured wisdom, of inspired talent and supreme compassion, could — no, shall — give to man a new sense of purpose in life just as soon as he is ready to ask for it. He could ask for it now.

The bottomless pit of despair, the unending path of frustration, the confused jungle of conflicting ideas, the chapters of savagery, of pain, of tears and blood, the dark nights of fear and torment, could all be melted into a forgotten yesterday.

This severance with restricting ignorance could be complete and absolute. A new morn, made light by the stream of higher knowledge, is withheld from our grasp because of our mechanical refusal to let go of our restrictions.

"Ask and it shall be given unto you," we are told. But in a mechanical response, we refuse to ask and refuse to prepare ourselves for the answer. To quote old wisdom again,there is a Spanish proverb which says, "What is it that you will have of life?" quoth the Gods. "Take it. Take it and pay for it."

163

The obvious question now, of course, is, "What is the price that we are required to pay in order that the higher and fuller promise of Spiritualism becomes a living reality?"

The effort of asking for knowledge and preparing ourselves to receive the answer is the payment for fulfilling our potential. Paying the right price is what too many Spiritualists are just not willing to do.

I suggest that before we can begin to think of the higher promise of Spiritualism, we should work at doing a much better job with the first objects of communion: that is to comfort the bereaved, and give evidence to the student. So let us improve our mediumship.

Ironically, mediumship, which was meant to liberate us from the mechanical order of life, has itself become too mechanical. And so, in the name of spirit communication, we are given evidence of psychic talent. At the signal of the chairman (usually after the more mechanical than inspiring rendering of a hymn) the medium will "switch on."

While switched on, he is expected to rattle off names and numbers, resolve problems and predict that "all will be well." He is expected to remain "switched on" until the chairman gives the "switch off" signal. This is usually given when it is time for the medium or congregation to catch a bus, train or television programme.

What sort of mediumship is that? The medium is here, not to be a puppet, dangled upon the whim or fancy of popular demand. He is here to fulfil an urgent and fundamental need — a need which existed before the arrival of the audience or congregation. The need is for each one attending to learn at his own pace that he is the spirit operating the machine. He needs to learn to take care of the machine which refines and develops that spirit through its lifetime on earth. One way to teach that is to demonstrate life after death. Another is to teach the spirit life within the material life.

So let us improve our mediumship. Let us encourage and train and evaluate our mediums.

Mediums require constructive criticism, but not necessarily from marketing managers (or any other individuals) who wish them to appeal to the greatest possible number of the public. To render the service required of him, the valuable critic must be able not only to penetrate into the technique of the medium, but also to perceive beyond it.

There is a desperate need for criticism and evaluation which can give a true and unbiassed account of the medium's work. We need people who know what happens in mediumship; people who will not be fettered by what certain others would want to happen. Emotion and feeling have their part to play in this, but so too do knowledge and understanding of the process. The critic should speak with the true voice of authority, and that voice should be of those who play no small part in this experiment between two worlds: it should be the voice of spirit.

I say this, because Spiritualism and spirit communication is not a business. It is a religion, an approach to God. As such, it requires humility on behalf of its participants. Those involved in mediumship (be they mediums, trainers or recipients) must have a deep sense of dedication, a great intensity of effort and a complete disregard for popularity or reward. Constancy of purpose must be theirs. These are the characteristics of the mediumship of liberation: the mediumship which teaches the freedom of the spirit to use the human machine to its fullest and highest potential.

The man who is able to commune with his own inner being is ready to commune with higher intelligences. He is ready to breathe into his soul the living breath of God.

The man who is able to commune with all being is the ultimate product of the human machine, and the perfect master of it.

The voice of such a man speaks with new authority. It is an authority of a breathing, feeling, knowing, living soul. Bravely he frees himself from the bondage of herd, tribe, mob and mass. No longer for him the meaningless role of a soul-less machine.

Never again will he be compared with the cold, sad earth which neither knows nor cares what is to become of it. Boldly now he declares his private fears, his hopes and his dreams so that at last the mechanical order gives way, and the new order of natural mediumship takes over. Such a man who finds the power of himself, finds too the power, wisdom, love and compassion of other souls.

Mediumship such as this ripens the moment for Spiritualism

to play its rightful part in the history of the world. It was Walter Scott who said, "We build our ideals out of snow, and then we weep to see them melt." Spiritualism has the power to change that epitaph upon the story of the human race.

For too long we have wallowed in hypocrisy and become entangled with outdated ideas. Let us with courage and vision tread now the path made open by a Spiritualism founded upon natural mediumship, a Spiritualism which can give us an understanding of the nature of our real self, which enables us to look within, so that with clearer seeing eyes, we may then gaze out.

Then perhaps we may feel as Carlyle when he wrote: "Man is of the earth, but his thoughts are one with the stars. Mean and petty his wants and desires; yet they serve a goal exalted with grand and glorious aims — with immortal longings — with thoughts which sweep the heavens, and wander through eternity. A pigmy standing on the outward crest of this small planet, his far-reaching spirit stretches outward to the infinite, and there alone finds rest."

Chapter Twenty

MILESTONES OF PHILOSOPHY

I HAVE lived in a mining village all my life. If you were to come along for a visit, the people there would soon take an interest in you and "size you up." Of course, they would take you for what you were and base their opinions on what they saw of you.

But before long they would be asking you what you did, where you come from and who your parents were. It's their way of sketching in your background and putting you in context so that they have a clearer picture of you.

Now such an approach isn't peculiar to the people of Troedyrhiw. They probably share this instinctive approach with the majority of interested human beings. We enjoy getting to know people as they are now, but we always feel we know them better when they have shared their history with us. We are suspicious of people who seem to have sprung up from nowhere.

The same is true of ideas. We like to know where they have come from and how they have evolved. We need to find out how they relate to the knowledge we already have. Until we know these things, we find them hard to understand and difficult to use: until then they do not become part of our lives.

As a visitor to today's community of religious thought, Spiritualism often raises more than a little suspicion. He seems to have sprung up from nowhere with a few unusual tricks to perform. The general attitude seems to be that the entertainer is just passing through and won't stay long, but this is ill-founded. It would be a good idea for the community to spend a little more time with its visitor, to find out more about his history, his vocation and how he links to themselves. He has plenty to tell.

167

People from many ages have been Spiritualists, although they may not accede to the name.

On their paths to God they have paused and reflected at many milestones which have pointed to a belief in the spiritual nature of man: many philosophers whose achievements have assured them they are going in the right direction. I call these stopping off points "Milestones of Philosophy," and because they mark the way Spiritualist thought has come. I would like to consider a few of them.

Let us flick back through the pages of history until we find ourselves in the tenth or eleventh century BC. Here we shall discover Homer, the reputed author of the legend of Troy. His epic poems are the oldest surviving specimens of European language. He based them on the accumulated traditions of past glories and valorous deeds rich with the joy of life and the dignity of man.

Homer captured the imagination of the Greeks to such an extent that his work became the sacred writings of the Greeks who came to believe that every word was true and inspired from heaven. The writings of Homer were so significant to the people of his time because he presented man at his most glorious, most heroic, most positive. He must have had the effect of raising the people's confidence in the abilities of mankind. His work was a tonic to read, encouraging the people as he did to "go out and do likewise." He was inspiring.

It is that inspiration which links this great writer to our present-day beliefs. We believe in progress. We believe we have all time in which to achieve it. Like his heroes, we need never give up. This highly positive attitude to crises, disasters and everyday life is integral to every thinking Spiritualist.

But the link between Spiritualism and ancient writings such as this is not limited to a shared attitude. Trace your fingers searchingly over the pages of history and you will always find that each fresh attainment of man is invariably attributed to a power above and beyond man. Heroes are helped by the Gods, by a power which flows from the realm called heaven.

Three thousand years on, Spiritualists refuse to forget that there is a power beyond themselves which acts upon their lives. Instead they endeavour to become more aware of that power in all its forms, to relate to it and to enable the flow to regenerate the glorious nature of man until it reaches heroic proportions once more. Man is only as mean or petty as he allows himself to be.

Move on three centuries or so, and we find our significant milestones all clustered together. One of the first indications of a golden age to come was the birth of Thales in Greece around about 640 BC. Thirty years on, he was followed by Anaximander, who tried to understand the material substance which made up the universe. He concluded that all such substance came from a single element which contained and governed all things.

His conclusion is mystical in nature, and close to contemporary Spiritualist thought which states that all things are expressions of spirit, and that spirit directs and controls all things.

Anaximander's one element was immortal and imperishable — just like the spirit we talk of two and a half thousand years later. The pedigree of our thought reaches far back into time. It is true to say though that surprisingly enough it does not conflict with the discoveries made by those involved in today's new physics.

In 600 BC with the birth of Xenophanes, we have another milestone, another example of pioneering thought. Xenophanes attacked Homer and all his works because his myths and legends with their plethora of all-too-human gods led away from objective reality. Such stories were entertaining and may have been symbolic, but they were also confusing.

As Christ was later to look beyond the stories of the Old Testament and cast them aside in favour of a simple, uncluttered philosophy, so Xenophanes attacked the theological myths and legends of his time to clear the way for a more rational school of thought. He established the Eleatic school of philosophy and taught:

1. There is only one God.

2. God is the mind which orders the universe. He is not a person.

3. God is the mental creation of each individual. As you are, so is your God.

4. God is beyond human comprehension.

5. There is unity in Nature: all is one and the One is God.

6. No God came to earth to suffer and die and rise again for

the sins of humanity.

This last point might seem strange, being expressed as it was 600 years before the appearance of Christ, but there have been other saviour gods such as Bel, Osiris, Prometheus, Mithra and Krishna.

It is, however, this last point which makes the Spiritualist approach so significantly different from the Christian one. Xenophanes denies that any god suffered and died to atone for the sins of men. He insists that God is much more than a human being, and cannot be meaningfully expressed through one; and that one individual cannot "pay" for the sins of another.

Spiritualist teaching agrees with this second point most heartily. It states that each individual is ultimately responsible for his own actions. "Yes," says the Spiritualist, "there is only one God." In designating him "Father," the Spiritualist credits the God Force with the creative and directive principle. It therefore follows that God must be beyond human comprehension because his powers are too vast for our limited minds to grasp.

"As above, so below" is a spiritual law frequently expounded by spirit teachers though their mediums. In this way, we can "see the universe in a grain of sand," as Blake wrote, "and eternity in an hour." If God is in us, and we are part of Nature, then it follows that God is in Nature too. In this sense of having God in common, all Nature must be one. Once again, the wisdom of past ages is reflected in our contemporary thought.

It intrigues me that our view of God is really a reflection of our own true natures. Suffice it to say that an all-knowing, all-loving God is the God of all philosophers through all the ages who have sought for the good and the true.

"One God, one law, one element, And one far off divine event, To which the whole creation moves," wrote Tennyson last century, in total harmony with his forebear, "Yet I doubt not through the ages one increasing purpose runs, And the thoughts of men are widened with the process of the suns."

But our path continues, this time in India. Up to the age of 29, Siddartha was a good-looking young prince who lived in great comfort and luxury. He had never known anything else.

When he finally did come in contact with poverty and

disease, old age and suffering — a life so different from all he had ever known — he turned his back on his lifestyle and all his possessions. From that time on, the story goes, he went out into the world alone, clothed in rags, determined to understand the reasons for suffering in life.

Like so many of the great figures of history, one of the first things Buddha did was to gather pupils around him. He taught them philosophy, born of his own experience. All the misery of life he traced to selfishness. The craving for individuality and the torment of greed bred unhappiness, he said.

To those who followed him, he taught that there was some-thing beyond earthly pleasure, something beyond earthly desires. By renouncing these pleasures and desires, and undertaking con-templation, he taught, a truer reality could be found. So, like all monks and nuns, he withdrew himself from the world to practise what he preached.

He comes down to us as one of the world's greatest philo-sophic pioneers. He encourages selfless service in us, and stand-ards which promote moral values. In his Aryan Path or Eightfold Way of Right Thinking and Right Acting, he outlines the ground rules for spiritual growth. They speak to us today whether we are Buddhist or Christian, Humanist or Spiritualist.

1. He insisted on truth and the abandonment of superstitions.

2. He insisted on the holding of right views and right aspirations because as base cravings are expelled, love of service for others takes their place.

3. Devotion to knowledge.

4. Devotion to right speech.

5. Devotion to right conduct.

6. Devotion to right living.

7. Devotion to right effort (one must not be lazy).

8. Right rapture.

We could, with considerable advantage, remind ourselves at various stages of our psychic and spiritual development of the Eight Rules of Buddha.

Spiritualism is often confused with a great interest in spirit people. Of course they are important. At the early stage of our understanding we rely on spirit people to prove their continued existence to us. Later we become concerned with spirit teachers and the techniques for developing psychic awareness and receiving communication from Spirit. But once Spiritualism has taught the immortal nature of spirit, its aim is to develop that spirit, to bring spiritual development to each individual. Buddha's instructions help us to understand how this can best be achieved.

His profound effect upon Eastern thought is reflected in this extract from sacred writings for the East. It is a wonderful example of clear insight into the real nature of man:

"The intelligent being in man from who all thought, desires, sweet odours and tastes proceed — he is myself within the heart who never speaks and is never surprised. He also is myself smaller than a corn of rice, smaller than a grain of mustard seed, yet greater than the earth, greater than the heaven, greater than all these worlds."

Near enough to the birth of Buddha (551 BC to be exact) there was born in China a man named Confucius. He was born at a time when China, due to wars and bad rulers, was in a condition of chaos. He set out to find a way of solving his country's difficulties of self-government, only to discover that his fellow countrymen were too ignorant and their rulers too selfish and stupid to heed his advice.

Like Buddha, he set about teaching. He established an academy to teach boys the principles of good conduct and right government. Here are two of his precepts:

1.   If the ruler is good and virtuous, the people will be likewise. (He stressed the power of example.)

2.   By education almost anything can be achieved.

Confucius would not abandon the cause of the people, and held his way to the end of his life, even although the princes of China spurned his advice. Apart from the success he achieved at Chung-tu, when he was allowed to take up the position of chief magistrate, his life on the whole was one of disappointment. He passed on as a tired, old man with the feeling that his life had not fulfilled its mission. It was only when he had gone that the Chinese people discovered his wisdom.

The finest thing education can teach us is how to learn. Once we know how to learn, all knowledge is potentially ours, and anything can be achieved. We only fully understand something when it becomes a meaningful part of our own experience. Then we have "had our education." We have truly learned.

Picture a teacher moving amongst his disciples. Picture in his arms a sheaf of madonna lilies, each perfect in every aspect. Each flower represents knowledge. As he walks among them, his students reach out towards him to receive a lily. He extends one to each, and it is theirs.

Watch him as he continues on his way, and you will be surprised. For although he gives a flower to each, his armful never diminishes. It is no miracle. Watch as his student reaches towards it, and just as contact is about to be made, his own flower of truth appears in his hand. The teacher continues on his way, having inspired the student to strive for and to attain, his own understanding.

Sometimes life is our teacher, sometimes we are taught by a friend, enemy or stranger. We may even teach ourselves, for a true teacher need only indicate two things: there is something to be learned here, and it is possible for you to learn it

With such encouragement, you do all the rest by reaching out to grasp the new mystery.

Spiritualist beliefs are firstly based on the messages of mediums. "There is something to learn about yourself here," they say. "Learn that you are a spiritual as well as a physical person." Then churches, communities, books, guides and friends say, "It is possible for you to learn all about it." Your own curiosity and determination to know does all the rest. Then, with Confucius, you share the knowledge that with such education, anything can be achieved.

In our own day and age, it is difficult to teach about Spirit on a grand scale because people's basic education is lacking. This is not necessarily their fault. It is just that general education today is more likely to deny the immortal self rather than to promote it. You can hardly make an apple pie if you don't believe you have any apples.

How can young people make anything of their spiritual selves when they don't even know if they have one? It is easy to turn Confucius' maxim on its head and say, "Without education almost nothing can be achieved." Spiritualists need to explain and demonstrate more than most people because they have in their listeners hardly any foundations from which to build. In fact, they may have to encourage others to "unlearn" some of their received wisdom before they can begin to make progress.

For example, it is surprising the number of people who have to get rid of the idea that spirit communication is the work of the devil, or somehow wrong, before they can be free to explore the variety of philosophy which opens up before them. However, despite the huge challenge on our hands, we still have much to thank Confucius for. We are duty bound to teach by example — and hope that the example is good enough!

With education of the young in mind, the Lyceum Manual was compiled by the early pioneers of Victorian Spiritualism. Emma Hardinge Britten, Alfred Kitson and H A Kersey drew from all religions and cultures to provide material which, in 1887 when the book was first published, they hoped would "aid in the promulgation of truth and the spiritual unfoldment of humanity." There is no one book or teacher that the Spiritualist in search of deeper understanding and spiritual experience restricts himself to. In this way he is able to claim many philosophers as his own, simply because they help him on his way.

We have already remarked upon the earlier Greek milestones of Thales, Anaximander and Xenophanes. Anaximenes, in 528 BC, endeavoured to trace the story of the material universe to its beginning. Anaximenes reiterated Anaximander's idea of all matter being composed from one element, but went further to say that that one element was air.

Today our own science with its complicated instruments and equipment may laugh at the simplicity of his suggestion, but in common with much religious thought, he was aware of the connectivity and one-ness of things. Early Spiritualists talked of this undifferentiated substance or energy as ether. This is defined in the dictionary as, "Substance of great elasticity and subtlety which has been postulated by wave-theory of light as permeating the whole of space and filling the interstices between particles of air and other matter."

Anaximander held that this one element rarefied and condensed into the material of the universe. In the same way, a Spiritualist will say of the soul that life's experience purifies and heightens the awareness of the conscious being within the body — the soul. Our "soul science" today is as naive perhaps as Anaximander's physical science was in his time, but having said that, it serves as a starting-off point for the next development, and must serve us until we can know more.

Anaxagoras approached his theory of matter from the opposite point of view. He started off with everything being different. The universe of an infinite number of seeds of different kinds of matter. In the beginning, these seeds were in a state of chaos, but with the advent of intelligence, a rotary impulse was given to the mass, and as a result, all cognate seeds gradually came together to form the different substances.

He was condemned in his day as atheistic for suggesting that the sun and the moon were not divinities but merely fiery lumps in the sky. But then anyone who wishes to express new ideas will inevitably have to reach out beyond the old, accepted wisdom, and is more than likely to meet with disapproval — as Spiritualists sometimes still do today.

Whatever his theology, Anaxagoras offers us the significant notion that intelligence can bring order out of chaos, and even produce new substance. In our own spiritual science, we respect the principle of eternal progress. That progress is the development of the spirit from unconscious, unformed energy into a highly individual and conscious force that I would call soul. The more conscious it becomes, the more like God it becomes, the more it expresses that consciousness, the more individual it becomes. It is through this creative use of consciousness, through intelligence, that such progress can be made, as Anaxagoras first suggested.

If you gaze down the long road of history and look upon the milestones of philosophy and notice that two of these milestones have a brilliance all of their own, they will be the milestones of Socrates and Plato.

Socrates was born in 470 BC. He suffered and was a martyr because he was courageous enough to speak his mind, to make known his honest thoughts. In his day, these did not always appeal to the state authorities. He did not travel much, but once at Delphi he saw the words "Know Thyself" inscribed on the door of a temple. From that time onwards, he set about the great task of learning to know himself.

By the same dialectical method of thesis, antithesis and synthesis, he questioned and analysed his way into finding the dualities which made for goodness, kindness, sympathy, truth, happiness, bravery and justice. To him the greatest virtue was pure knowing, and he would accept nothing that would not pass the acid test of reason.

Socrates is the prime example of what our approach to Spiritualism and spiritual development must be. It is too easy to say "Yes" to a medium's message and to accept in a sloppy sort of way that she might have proved life after death to you. That is no good if you want to move out of the realms of hapless faith or superstition and into some more reasoned reality.

"Do not fear precision," say the authors of the Lyceum Manual. "It is more conducive to grace than a slipshod, careless manner."

Having received messages as lovingly as we can, we should review them later with reasoned question and analysis. The same is true of any philosophy given by a teacher or through a medium. It has to withstand rational questioning for if it cannot, it can be of little help to us on our path to a greater understanding of life and ourselves.

For insisting on this reasoned approach, and allegedly undermining the youth of his day, Socrates was condemned to death by drinking hemlock.

Prior to his death, he was asked by his friend Crito, "How shall we bury you?" to which he replied: "Wherever you may, if only you can catch me. Is it not strange that after all I have said to convince you that I am going to the society of the happy, you still think this body to be Socrates? To die and be released is better for me." There is no doubt that Socrates shared the Spiritualist belief in life after death, and the Spiritualists' problem of convincing other people that they mean what they say!

To think or speak of Socrates is to think or speak of Plato (427 BC) for it was in the company of Socrates that Plato spent many of his early days. It is generally agreed that Plato was one of the world's greatest thinkers. His works have become monuments of literature. He opened a school called the Academy. It was from there that intellectual light penetrated a dark world of ignorance.

There seems to be something of Plato in every great or noble utterance. In fact, the wisdom of all ages and climes seems contained in this one superior mind. Every word and thought that flowed from his lips and pen has its own immortality and timelessness. Let me remind you of the invitation this king of philosophy extends to you and me and all humanity:

"I am therefore persuaded by these accounts, and consider how I may exhibit my soul in a healthy condition. Wherefore, disregarding the honours that most men value, and looking to the truth, I shall endeavour to live as virtuously as I can, and when I die, to die so; and I invite all other men to the utmost of my power to this contest which, I affirm surpasses all contests here."

We often talk of life's challenges, but how often do we consider that to die well is the greatest of life's challenges? It seems a contradiction in terms, a denial of all that life is about. It seems a denial only because we see death as the annihilation of life. It is not. It is a rite of passage, a developmental change, a transition. Seen in this way, it becomes an achievement. To allow the best possible achievement, preparation has to be made. The ultimate success of this life is not dependent on chance or good fortune, but on the growth of the soul.

Why is this so? Because in this life, the physical body is the vessel for the learning and loving soul. As the vessel journeys though the world of its years, the soul is offered endless opportunity for response. As it responds, it grows. As the soul grows and its vessel ages, the individual as we know him should have become more understanding and loving. The more he becomes loving and understanding, the more he is prepared for life in the non-physical. If he is prepared in this way, then death is "virtuous" (morally excellent).

In those few words, Plato has sketched the outline of the aim and purpose of what we call Spiritualism today. We emphasise we have a spirit which lives on beyond the body's life to encourage first and awareness of that spirit, and secondly a nurturing of that spirit so that it can live in or be exhibited in a healthy condition.

177

This is the process of preparing for death as Plato speaks of it — not preparing for annihilation, but for the fuller spiritual life and a greater reality.

Homer, Thales, Anaximander, Xenophanes, Anaximenes, Socrates, Plato — these are only a few of the philosophers produced by Greece. What does it mean to a country to have so many great thinkers?

Well, the Greeks were among the first people to live a national life. Besides the national games which united the people, the Greeks had a common language. They also worshipped the same gods. As in China, the father of the household was the family priest.

It seems to me that thought is the motive power behind progress, and that one man's thought provides the environment which makes possible the thought of many others. The thought of many others then advances as the civilisation of which it is a part. When a group or a society or a nation allows freedom of thought through education, that group is saying, "We are ready to progress," and "We are confident enough to face change."

The result of this attitude is more understanding, more knowledge, an ever-widening culture. This is what a history of thinkers means to a country. It does not mean a uniformity or a sameness, but the full diversity and variety which is reflected is Nature itself.

The Greeks developed a personal and not a state religion. Each individual worshipped the gods as he thought right for himself. Similarly, each thinking Spiritualist is accorded the responsibility of working out and following his own spiritual pathway, using whatever sources of help he sees fit.

When the Greeks were in need of help or comfort, they went to one of the two hundred oracles (or mediums) who lived in the temples and shrines throughout the land. Thus they discovered what they termed the will of God, just as the adherents of the Apostolic Church at a later date believed that the Holy Spirit controlled the medium who spoke in trance or passed on what they saw clairvoyantly at their church services.

In an attempt to make a living, some of our mediums today use their talents in demonstrations which are little short of stage shows. Although skilled in their abilities, there seems to be little here that is spiritual, educational or inspiring. But before we become too hearty in our condemnation of contemporary mediums, we should look more closely at ourselves and the superficial interest we take in them.

If we want the best from our mediums, we must give them the best. If we want their work to be spiritual, we must educate and train them in spiritual things. We don't expect concert pianists to develop from playing a piano in a pub. No. We send them to conservatories and Masters and pay them to practise so that we may wonder at their work. Nor do we expect them to be bakers or computer programmers by day and masters of music in their spare time.

We expect this of our mediums though, and it is to their credit that despite us, some work for the love of service and nothing more. And some do teach and advise, soothe and inspire in ways reflecting those of their Greek forebears. In this sense, Spiritualists walk the same path as the Greeks, but do not walk it as well. We must recognise that we can learn from the past for it is there that our heritage lies. Call it our inheritance if you will for one day we shall come of age and grow ready to accept it.

It is startling to look back and see that what is relatively new to our civilisation (Modern Spiritualism is said to have begun with the experiences of the Fox sisters in 1848), was well understood thousands of years ago. What happened to that understanding, and why has a personal awareness of spirit fallen into religious disrepute within our own culture? After all, until 1951, mediumship was, strictly speaking, a criminal offence.

Of all the difficulties that philosophy has met, there can be no doubt that the greatest has been the Christian Church. By that I do not mean the teachings of Jesus. In the exposition of love and charity, the nature of God and man's relation to him, he is matchless. While Greek thought specialised in the objective art of knowing, Jesus' teaching provides the other side of the coin (so to speak), the subjective side of loving.

Knowing and loving are the two functions of being: the one enhances and completes the other. Yet the Christian Church condemned all knowledge beyond the Biblical and doctrinal, and in doing so negated the love it was supposed to be propounding. Instead of knowledge continuing to spread as it had done for the proceeding 600 years, a black curtain of ignorance descended upon the most virile portion of the human race.

All efforts to raise the people to a higher level become of no account: old and new teachings alike were denounced as the work of the devil. Knowledge was regarded as sinful. Ignorance was elevated to the rank of a virtue. The Church, as something akin to a factory of ignorance, supported itself by its clergy taking 10 per cent of all that the land produced, imposing a further burden on a now restricted people.

This long, dark night was probably the greatest tragedy of our civilisation. It caused suffering which today seems like some dream that could not have been true. Men in power then went to such lengths to impose their views on the rest of mankind that they make Hitler seem quite ordinary. It may seem hard for us to believe, yet it is all too terribly true that in its bid to shut out real knowledge and force men to accept Christian theology, over 25 million people were ruthlessly slain by the Church and its agents.

Here and there, of course, arose men whose standard of culture, whose minds, could not be entirely held down. These men's moral courage compelled them to give to the world what knowledge came their way. Such men paid dearly for their courage, and very few had any worthwhile success for the tremendous sacrifices they made. However, no matter how severe repression or tyranny might have been, eventually by the law of life, a reaction set in.

An indication of such a reaction can be seen in Francis Bacon, who was born in 1561 AD. He is called the father of experimental philosophy. In his time, he advocated the formation of a corporate body devoted to the study of science. This idea ultimately materialised in the reign of Charles the Second when the Royal Society for Scientific Investigation was formed. This was an event which was to stimulate an outlook on life which was so revolutionary that the old way of thinking and living was entirely changed.

We can perhaps gain some idea as to the standard of the ethics of the Christians of that era when we note that Bacon was the first Christian of any rank to maintain that a Christian or a Christian government was morally bound to keep an agreement with a non-Christian individual or government.

The effect of Bacon was that gradually the broader, fuller and more intelligent way of life became open again. Due to the climate he helped to create, there arose men whose mental ability and spiritual consciousness refused to remain imprisoned. Knowledge once more began to see the light of day.

You will remember the brave attempts of Xenophanes to raise the people above the superstitions of their time. The Christian Church put the clock of progress back 2,400 years for we have to wait until the 18th century for Voltaire to follow in the steps of this famous Greek philosopher. Voltaire scoffed at the Christian mythology and theology. He emphasised once more the unity of God and Nature. In consequence, he was expelled from Paris and forced to find refuge abroad.

The same difficulties were met by any who wished to interpret religion in their own way or experience a personal oneness with spirit, whether it be the spirit of all or communion with the spirit of another individual. The knowledge and wisdom of the past had become heresies which had to be destroyed before they led to destruction. Despite this, however, one by one, men who were poets, men who were scientists, men who were destined to become social and religious leaders, arose and took hold once more of the truth which so long ago had been attained by mankind.

As one by one, leading minds of the eighteenth and nineteenth centuries shook themselves free from the chains of theological creeds and systems, and sought for truth and fact which could stand the test of logic and scientific investigation, the way was prepared for new and wider horizons in science, philosophy and religion.

The aim of these thinkers was to find a science, philosophy and religion which not only took hold of all that was best in the philosophy and religion of all lands and ages prior to the establishment of Christianity, but also to blend these three threads together and add to them so that they would take on a meaning more fresh and real than anything our civilisation had ever known.

However, you cannot just "find" a science. It cannot fall out of the air at you, like an apple drops from a tree. A science is a set of principles drawn from a body of knowledge. That body of knowledge will have been built up from a long time of practical experience. It will have been recorded because the information will have been seen to be useful and helpful in everyday life. In other words, there was a need for that information. Let me explain what I mean.

Man needs food. He eats berries, nuts and seeds as he finds them in Nature. He needs more food as his family and community grows. He notices that Nature re-seeds herself each year, so he plants seeds, sometimes in the right soil, sometimes at the wrong time of year. Gradually, through trial and error, he learns the best places to plant his seeds, and the best time of year to do it. He learns the need for fertiliser, for watering, for fallow years and so on. As the body of knowledge grows, it needs to be organised and systematised if he is to find easily what he is looking for, and to understand how this fits in with the rest of his knowledge of life.

It is at this point that the thinker, the philosopher, plays his part. Someone has to review the body of knowledge and identify the significance therein. It requires the keen eye and an ability to see the general picture or overview before general principles can be identified, but it is only then that a system is imposed upon the knowledge , the principles (of for example, agriculture) are identified and the science (of agriculture) is born.

No sooner does this happen than people become experts in particular areas, like soils or root crops, animal husbandry or the accurate measurement of times and seasons. Before you know it, knowledge from experience of a variety of specialist areas grows, requires systematisation, and science gives birth to new sciences: geology, horticulture, veterinary science, chronology and so on.

Knowledge begets knowledge as thought begets thought. We have already seen that the Greeks had so many thinkers because their first thinkers provided the environment for more thought and therefore more thinkers. The role of environment cannot be overstated. Thus once scientific thought becomes established, it will promote more and more scientific thought, scientists and science.

Man is never content for long with his improved lot. He soon recognises new needs, devises new experiences and develops new sciences in turn. Look how man's achievement of air travel led to the challenge of space flight. In a few short years, the new sciences of electronics, computing and new physics exploded into being. Once there is a need, there will soon be a new science, for science is man's attempt to fulfil his needs.

While man's experience is limited in a sphere of life, and his body of knowledge is too sketchy to make much sense of, he will relegate that area to the unexplained: it's "just life" or "God's will." We still credit God or fate with the control of disasters, sudden death, unexplained disease, coincidence, happy chance and bad luck. If we have a religious nature, we will pray for protection against the worst of these, and quiet resignation if they do befall us.

We pray about these things because we have no science to apply to them (yet). In contrast, most of us today would not leave the chances of a good crop to prayer. Instead we would apply all the best of our scientific knowledge to our land and seeds, knowing that only the weather was not solely "in the hands of God."

What we do not understand then, we give a religious explanation for. When we understand it a little more, we are in a position to surmise about it. This is where the philosopher takes over, as I have already remarked. By making imaginative leaps, he strives to see order in the apparent chaos so that man can begin to understand and then control his experience. When, in time, experience proves the philosopher to be correct, his philosophy becomes a new science. When he is proved wrong, his work is recognised only as a fantasy, but it may not be entirely dismissed because it has played an important part in the discovery of the truth.

The Spiritualists of the late nineteenth century and early twentieth, were quick to accept that the contemporary upsurge of psychic phenomena was the experience which proved the philosophers of old to be in fact the first spiritual scientists. Robert Owen, through the mediumship of Emma Hardinge Britten, gave what came to be the Seven Principles of Modern Spiritualism. Drawing from the philosophies of old, these principles helped to systematise them, bringing into focus the possibilities of a new science which would be the science of spirit.

As psychic phenomena became recognised as true by many great scholars, the philosophy arising out of the implications of these phenomena was born. This new wave of intellectual growth spread itself over all the most enlightened parts of the world. Such men as Sir William Crookes, Alfred Russell Wallace, Sir Oliver Lodge, Sir William Barrett in England, Dr Ryston and Professor William James in America, Lombroso, Flammarion and Charles Richet in Europe, all became interested in psychic phenomena. Most of them henceforth devoted themselves to the establishment of this new philosophy.

Up and down our land, men and women met for the purpose of holding experimental circles to prove for themselves that the religious practice of peoples who had dwelt in distant lands in a now dim and obscured past were based upon a living reality. As a result of those circles, contact was often made with intelligences who had once walked this way. And because of these contacts and the communications which followed, an entirely new system of science and philosophy was evolved.

The new science awaited the firm establishment of the "new" philosophy. Churches were built from which these new teachings could be proclaimed in the name of Spiritualism. Once more people could practise their psychic and spiritual gifts. Societies were organised in order that the understanding and benefits of these great truths might spread their ways over all the earth.

More and still more works of philosophy were written as psychic and spiritual experiences added to the body of knowledge. Mediums found teaching flowing through them. The souls of poets were stirred into the production of new poetry and a deeper understanding of lines such as these of Wordsworth:

"Ever on the watch, willing to work
"And be wrought upon.
"They need not extraordinary calls
"To rouse them; in a world of life they live.
"By sensible impressions not enthralled
"But by their quickening impulses made more prompt
"To hold fit converse with the spirit world."

The Seven Principles of Spiritualism form the foundation of a philosophy which finds itself in harmony with the world's oldest and greatest teachings, setting alight once more the torch of knowledge which the organisation of the Christian Church by sheer brute force had extinguished. This torch, now relit, sheds its

184

beams and makes discernible to you and me not only the philosophical milestones of yesteryear, but also makes clear what could become the most significant milestone of all: the milestone marking the philosophy of tomorrow.

"Know Thyself" is the common instruction of Greek metaphysics. To know thyself, say these Greek scholars, is to know that you are of the One: the one law, the one cause, the one God. To the One, sooner or later, you will return.

"Forget Thyself" is the prescription of Indian thinkers who claimed that the way to salvation and truth can only be found in the stripping away of one's own individuality.

"Realise Thyself" is the Chinese adage. Realise thyself that Tao may be for you. Tao means the way, but the way used in this sense takes on a meaning more rich and full than in the common usage of our language. Their way is the way of life, the way of heaven, the ultimate being.

From the East and from the West, men of many lands and ages have passed this way gathering on their journey some threads of knowledge. In the process of gathering these threads, they have shed their earthly bodies, but the task to which they dedicated themselves continues: ever watchful, ever alert, ever eager to gather more and ever more of these threads of learning, they continued along their individual paths.

"Ask and it shall be given unto you," we are taught. "Seek and ye shall find." Some of those who are asking and searching find themselves upon similar paths and call themselves Spiritualists. They may be strange or strangers to some in the community of religious thought, but they are old friends to others.

Those with eyes that see, with imaginations which are alive, cannot fail to perceive the ultimate consequence of souls incarnate and discarnate meeting together in the peaceful hush of the home circle or in the sacred quiet of the church service or seance.

Here, where souls from East and West, past and present, gather together, here where men of the spiritual world meet and mingle with men still of earthly abode, here where souls of different culture join in etheric embrace; it is inevitable that a philosophy scaling higher loftier heights, reaching deeper depths than ever before, shall emerge.

From this boundless reservoir of knowledge is drawn wisdom which comes from some of the oldest and richest of ages. Thus with a vision more clear and a purpose more real, we can take hold again of Buddha's Eightfold Way, and tread the Aryan Path.

By our becoming good and virtuous and making practical use of education, Confucius will become less tired and will feel old and sad no more. Socrates, from the society of the happy, shall help us still to know ourselves, while Plato's republic based upon justice shall not forever remain a poetic dream, but will from its slumber arise into the glory of reality. The voice of Xenophanes will live again as one by one we recite our principles, reaffirming the teaching of this courageous Greek Scholar.

Our journey through life involves the process of discovering that which is true and becoming advised in the practice of that which is good. Voltaire says, "These are the two most important objects of philosophy." So to the milestone of tomorrow we slowly, somewhat painfully, move our way.

The body of thought which today goes by the name of Spiritualism should be allowed to take its place in the community of religious thought. It has its pedigree and its history, and if allowed to, could gently draw the strands of other religions closer together. It has its past, but it also has a future because it stands on the threshold of science.

Spiritual teachers have always offered to our intuition what our rational minds cannot explain. There are so many questions: What is the purpose of life? What is life? If there is a God, what is He and where is He? What is man? Does he have an aim?

These questions have not yet been answered to the satisfaction of reason. Because science has no conclusive response to offer, and philosophy has taken so long to suggest the best approach, answers to these questions have been left to religion. Religion in turn has had to ask its followers to have faith because certainty is in short supply.

Now this visitor called Spiritualism does not stroll into the community of religious thought with all the answers in his pack. He may claim that he is a scientist, but as yet that is not strictly true. If he works at it, he may be a scientist in the making, but just now it is philosophy and experience that he has in his pack.

That is what he has to share with his hosts. He knows the essence of life is spirit, that the aim of this life is to induce consciousness in that spirit. He knows that once awakened, the function of conscious spirit is to love and to know. He knows that when these two functions develop and blend, they are creative.

He understands that Spirit is evolving energy and that God is the sum total of that energy. In turn, this implies that all energy is an expression of God and that God is in all things.

To the philosopher he says, "Identify the laws of Spirit and you shall have identified the laws of life."

To the scientist he says, "Apply the laws of life and you can control life by working with it."

To the religious he says, "Live by the laws of life and you shall be at one with the God you know."

If only a fraction of the time, money and effort allocated to the other sciences were devoted to the science of the Spirit, the results would be revolutionary: religion, philosophy and science would permeate and complement each other creatively. However, at this time, in these limited circumstances, we survey the experiences of psychics, mediums and ordinary men that the Spiritualist has to offer, and we begin to identify trends, characteristics, coincidences which will lead to new systems and principles.

Some of our Spiritualist philosophy today will later be found to be fantasy, but if it is used as a starting point for experimentation, some of it will prove to be the beginning of the science of Spirit — the science of Life.

We may already have reached the most remarkable milestone of all.

Chapter Twenty One

CHANGES

ALL is movement, all is change. In 1951, I joined Hoovers and remained with them till the end of my working life in 1977. Looking back, life has been a tapestry of meetings, services, classes and lectures woven in and around ever-changing shifts and rotas. That is what life as a Spiritualist minister has meant to me.

To mark twenty-five years' service with Hoovers, I was invited, with some colleagues, to have a meal with the manager. He was interested to hear that Will Ford the line leader was also a minister. "What are you doing working here?" he asked. "I am a Spiritualist," I replied, "but I don't expect to make a living out of Spiritualism. That's not what it's for."

After all, is the gift not given freely? Should I not give too? There are rewards in giving, of course, in terms of the pleasure of people. I have met and worked with so many people through Spiritualism, both young and old. I was President of the South Wales District Lyceum for years. Later, I was President of the South Wales District Council from 1951 until 1976. During that time, we achieved a great deal, running and maintaining what was an international, annual Summer School. As you can see from the photograph, the schools were large-scale affairs, drawing people of all ages and persuasions.

We pioneered the group system where the district was subdivided into smaller groups of churches who met and worked together on a regular basis, establishing a community network of Spiritualists. This encouraged friendly competition and a healthy exchange of approaches and ideas. Without that kind of exchange, the life goes out of an organisation. Spiritualism should be a family with all the family members aware of the others, their ideas, their needs.

These two decades were busy years, good years, fruitful years. Looking back, I can see a scattering of seeds at that time. Seeds of ideas, seeds of hope, seeds of dreams. I and my generation of friends planted them with the help of Spirit. They are seeds for future growth, ready to sprout when the time and the environment are right. When things change.

If you and your generation of friends, with the help of Spirit, feel a stirring inside at the words you read, you may choose to nurture the ideas, hopes and dreams. You may tend their growth and harvest their fruit, and change things further.

For life is change. Change is life. We should never be surprised at how radically or suddenly our lives can change. One evening, a neighbour called at Park Place. "Katie!" I shouted. "Visitors!" Kate appeared unsteadily at the top of the stairs — she had taken a stroke. Its effects, for such an active and energetic woman, were highly frustrating. Yet with careful nursing and constant healing, she made a good recovery.

Our lives were changing. Early retirement to allow me more time with Kate, my writing and my garden, became an attractive prospect. It became a necessity in 1977, when Kate suffered a second, more severe stroke.

Over the last ten years of her life, the world became a smaller place for Kate and I, but hardly a quieter one. I withdrew from most of my public work, but I am glad to say our friends did not withdraw from us. Visits and letters brought an added brightness to the fireside. And whereas action was once the order of the day, reflection now takes priority!

Chapter Twenty Two

INTERPENETRATIVE PHILOSOPHY

O YE who sit and gaze on life
With folded hands and fettered will,
Who only see amid the strife
The dark supremacy of ill,
Know that like bird and stream and flowers
The life that moves you is divine!
Nor time, nor space, nor human powers
Your God-like spirit can confine.
God of the granite and the rose!
Soul of the sparrow and the bee!
The mighty tide of being flows
Through all thy creatures back to Thee.
Thus round and round the circle runs,
A mighty sea without a shore
While men and angels, stars and suns,
Unite to praise Thee evermore.

"God of the granite and the rose" is still a popular hymn in Spiritualist churches. Ironically, in its opening lines, it reflects exactly the situation of the modern Spiritualist who looks gloomily upon life, forgetting the unlimited potential that is his. Thankfully, the closing lines remind him of his essential limit-less-ness.

The Seven Principles of Spiritualism extend far beyond their apparent simplicity. In fact, they form a spiritually inspiring interpenetrative philosophy. Once this is understood, we can begin to see what needs to be done to ensure a positive future for Spiritualism.

So much of life surrounds us at every hand, yet so much of life remains unknown. Of life's many enigmas, the greatest one is that of human nature. Having evolved through many realms and forms of life, of which so much still remains unknown, abiding in a present which we can ill define, moving towards and into a future which is indefinite, dim and obscure, human life remains the greatest enigma.

We need a philosophy drawn from life to help us cope with life itself. This philosophy, as we shall see, is Spiritualism.

SOCIETY — ITS RELATION TO PHILOSOPHY

Such is the material of society that despite the indefinite, unknowable nature of life, men are forever building and rebuilding their hopes: planning and replanning, dreaming and redreaming.

Despite the clouds of obscurity, there still have arisen men to found society, to establish religion and to evolve science. Philosophy of life has been fashioned by men in an attempt to make more bright and helpful their portion here. The pioneers of Spiritualism did just this.

THE SUCCESS OF SOCIETY

There has been some considerable degree of success in the growth and development of society because of man's philosophical approach to life and its problems. We have had our poets, our men of vision, religious leaders, soul-illumined thinkers, men of brave heart, of courageous and noble purposes, men of science, men of larger heart and kindlier hand, men of true talent and of rich and pure character.

Triumphant and wondrous are the achievements of a society that is forever being startled by new and strange discoveries; high are the mounts unto which human endeavour soars. Great indeed are the blessings and benefits they bring down to human kind.

No Spiritualist today would deny that the seminal philosophy of Spiritualism is a great achievement.

THE FAILURE OF SOCIETY

Alas, however, this measure of success is incomplete. We

can have no illusions of this society which is perilously dependent upon an unpredictable human nature. It is capable at any moment of sinking into action and behaviour more base, low and degrading than we ever believed possible, until by actual encounter we are shocked into an acceptance of an evil which is grim and real.

Complications are dealt with and overcome only to be replaced with newer and greater ones. Disease is conquered only to be followed by a disease more stark and terrible. Sweetest joys are soured by uncertainty. Fairest days are made dark by the gloom of insecurity. Men's fondest dreams do not come true.

Utopia is not attained; the age of peace is not reached. Justice, freedom and equality are words which mockingly taunt the victims of our most imperfect social order. Ever present is the fear that society may one day lie in a grave dug by its own unhealthy hand. There are times, too, when we fear we have failed Spiritualism.

THE RELATIONSHIP OF SOCIETY AND PHILOSOPHY BREAKS DOWN

This is the point where society and philosophy fall apart. Philosophy breaks down, defeated by human nature. Our first major problem is to discover the cause of this breakdown.

We shall divide life into two main groups: these two groups have been, and are, forever at war. This war we will call the war of the old and the new. One life is content with its present way and the way of yesterday: the other life urges change and would make tomorrow today.

To understand this position, we must try to bear in mind the path we have come and to realise that human life has not just suddenly existed, but has been in the process of becoming through many realms and forms of life for countless ages. The more highly evolved parts of our nature (or for that matter, all the attributes of life we have in one realm or kingdom of our evolution) do not just cease to be the moment we are promoted into another order of life. It is by constant toil and effort that these attributes have to be redirected and re-educated into their new sphere.

Life does not always enter into its new home gladly or willingly: there is protest, and the echo of this protest goes long and far into the new day. Thus still in so many humans is heard the yelp of the beast, still is heard the voice of the jungle.

So it is that the philosophy of Spiritualism breaks down because its supporters bring with them remnants of past beliefs and prejudices.

Philosophy breaks down because it is meant for a society of men and yet is written by and for a society of beings not wholly men; a society still in the process of becoming men, still in the process of being educated into a consciousness of their manhood.

THE PROBLEM AS APPROACHED BY SPIRITUALISM

Such then is the problem facing modern Spiritualism. It must tackle this problem by teaching its principles more thoroughly and by looking more closely at their detailed implications.

Its first principle is the Fatherhood of God. This is the basis of its philosophy. Let us try to trace some of the fuller and more important implications of this principle.

Fatherhood.

The first point we must grasp is if the Fatherhood is true, then all life is one. No other principle of any philosophy of any science or any religion can be true unless it is related to this one fact. All men who were, who are and shall yet be, are one. To be true to this philosophy, man must serve not only his needs and interests, but the needs and interests of all men: men of yesterday, today and tomorrow. That is only a small part of this all-important principle.

However, as man must also realise, he is one not only with all men, but with all forms of life from whatever realm or whatever kingdom. He must be actively aware of his direct relation to all things.

The logical sequence of this is that if all life is one, then all time is one. We must see that our whole conception of time values must change. A few days seem of little importance to humans, yet to a flower in bloom it means so much. The tempo of its life and of all plant life is much quicker: the whole time value is different.

You place your seed in the garden today. In a few weeks there is a seedling, a few more weeks a plant. A few more weeks again and it is in the fullness of its growth. In the mineral kingdom, we behold yet another completely different set of time values where hundreds, sometimes thousands of years might be just so many minutes as compared with human standards. Growth and change we can see in humans in a period of years, in plant life, weeks and months; in the mineral hundreds, sometimes millions, of years.

The Fatherhood then is unconcerned with time. Time just does not matter. Life is to become, to grow, to evolve; perchance today, perchance tomorrow, perchance millions of years hence. What does it matter when? Time in the philosophy based upon the Fatherhood is not this or that or any moment, but all moments. Spiritualism should be more concerned with becoming, less concerned with the image of now.

Brotherhood .

Brotherhood viewed in the light of the foregoing means much more than a society living peaceably and happily together. We are now dealing with that part of philosophy where everyone seems to understand what is required, but where all fail just to make the grade. It is at this point that the philosophy of Spiritualism would remind us that no principle, no ideal, can be understood or achieved if treated as a separate principle. If is be true that all life is one, then all principles are one.

When we would desire good results from our garden, we appreciate that certain preparations are necessary to the soil. So it is in the garden of human life. From the moment a soul is born into this life, this great preparation must begin. Whatever the hopes or dreams for thc new life may be, the first step must invariably be to prepare the soil of the soul. The physical body must be fed and cared for in order for it to become strong and healthy as a channel through which may manifest other higher attributes of life.

Thus the new life is taught the gospel of feeding. The old instinctive self protests strongly at the human method of feeding. Blindly, unknowingly, in previous orders of life there was but one law of its nature to be obeyed: to be itself, moved forward by change and grown by instinct. Unconscious and unaware, the stone was a stone, the plant a plant. Time would work its hand upon each, the elements of nature would decide for it its form, size, colour. It

194

could not choose or alter what it is. It had no say, no voice. There was instinct, but it did not know. It was unaware.

In the human realm, however, slowly and gradually there comes into being the attributes of the mental self. Life begins to know. It is aware. The instinctive self does not always accept its new master gladly and so the war of the old instinctive self and the new knowing self continues throughout the many phases of human life.

We must not treat these parts of our nature as distinct and separate parts. Let us bear in mind the basis on which we are working. All life is one. Each part must give and receive the other. For knowledge to penetrate, instinct is not enough. Each must penetrate the other. This interpenetrative must bind our different life forces and energies together into a lasting, indissoluble partnership.

We have pointed out the mental self is only just finding its way. The world, which moment by moment seems ever to widen, is strange. The people are strange and unknown, the way is strange, the things of life are strange and so fear is a very prominent feature of early human life. This remains so until experience slowly teaches the mental self that other men and other things are one in the Father, are one in them. Instinctive fear now grows or evolves into a conscious fear, not of but for other men.

This is a tremendous crisis in the growth and development of human nature, because not only does it indicate the beginnings of a real Brotherhood, but also it brings into evidence the spiritual part of man.

All the while this sense of brotherhood had been there, just as the colour and shape and form of the plant had all the while been in the seed, unable to show itself, unable to make known its presence until placed in properly prepared soil. Now, at long last, man is aware of man. Man is aware that he can serve man and by man be served. Man is aware of the earth and the things of the earth and more and more he finds them good. So the soil of the soul is prepared and is ready for man's higher or spiritual self to be announced.

In its endeavour to find for itself means for expression, the soul makes newer and heavier demands on the physical and mental self. Newer richer talents are brought into being. Greater methods employed. Higher systems evolved.

It is necessary at this stage for an adequate code of ethics to be evolved. Ethics was first evolved without there being anything spiritual or moral about it. This first moral code was a list of taboos. Things to be done, not because it would be good or virtuous, but because it would be profitable; things not to be done because it would be wrong or evil, but dangerous.

Throughout the evolution of ethics, there has always been, and there still remains, this notion of profit and loss, but in each succeeding stage of its development, there is clearly to be discerned more and ever more of the spiritual aim and a more God-like soul motive.

Brotherhood demands of each Spiritualist that he nurtures others and lives ethically for others.

The Immortality of the Soul.

It is at this point that the plans and the dreams of a happy world and a well organised society begin. Politics come into being and we are taught of its ideals. Here we witness the breaking down of social and political systems, the collapse of ideals, the fading of dreams, the vision melts ere we touch it.

In this all important crisis of the evolution of human life, it is vital for us to obtain a true picture of events. We must understand why after man evolves sufficiently to enquire, question and reason over problems of life and be able to quite a remarkable degree to give the answers to those questions, he is unable to make the right use of the knowledge which his searching, enquiring mind has acquired for him. Why, after receiving education in moral standards of life and of human behaviour is it that in actual life man falls so short of these standards? We see ourselves failing in this way in our churches.

Why, when we understand so much of what is required to make a truly great soul, when we know so well the value and worth of purity, nobility and grace, is it that there is, in actual fact, so much that is vile, low, cunning and brutal, heartless behaviour?

One thing only can have gone wrong. Our human preparation

is at fault. Bring in the architects and the builders. Tell them what you require of them, and apart from technical knowledge, materials, labour, etc., what else would they need?

Firstly, they would require space. Set a limit on the space, and you confine and restrict their ability to give you the necessary results.

Further, they would require time. The less time the builders are to be allowed, the less good may be the results you have the right to expect.

So it is in the larger field of life. The soul and mind of man, capable of dreaming high and noble dreams, capable of planning a pure, happy society, capable of wisdom, vision, capable of grappling with the secrets and problems of life, must have room enough to work. The ever-expanding, ever-growing soul and mind of man must not be restricted by lack of space in which to grow, expand, work and live.

Further, the aspiring, hungry, ambitious soul must have time. We must surely see that all the principles of all philosophy must be penetrated by this next principle of modern Spiritualism.

The Immortality of the Soul.

In embracing this truth, the minds and souls of men immediately are conscious of being alive in a larger world. There at once springs to life within their beings the awareness that their hopes, faiths, dreams, ambitions and ideals (however high, however noble, however much beyond their present ability) are possible and reachable. There is a purpose in life. There is purpose to every experiment. There is purpose in tears, in the pains and trials of life. Time for each experiment in its own day to declare its own true glory. Time for tears, pains and trials to earn their just reward.

Already we see hints of other principles. We feel this truth forcing its all powerful, mighty way into paths we had dared not walk. Conceptions of personal responsibility, or compensation and retribution of an entirely different hue, more grand and wonderful than anything we had thought possible, loom up and appear before us.

At last we have our finger on the very pulse of life's enigma.

197

It is here that education must succeed or else in all other departments meet with utter and complete defeat. It is here we see meaning and purpose in the ebb and flow of life, of the penetration and interpenetration of principles. This is the key which unlocks the door unto a truer and more wonderful conception of the Fatherhood, for now indeed the soul is aware of its immortality, knowing its deathless nature can exclaim, "All life is one, all time is one!" We must give each other time.

Communion of Spirit.

The conception of the principle of the world's immortality will only become just another unfulfilled purposeless vision and cause our ideals, our hopes and dreams to wither and, corpse-like, fall into the speechless, dreamless and silent dust unless we have at this vital point the necessary knowledge to nourish and vitalise our being. An idea or a faith, of themselves, must surely perish unless the mind can take hold of something evidential and be able to cry aloud, "This I know to be true!"

You will appreciate, therefore, how important it is to follow with our next principle — Spirit Communion. I always prefer the term "Divine communion."

Here again, unless there is proper and adequate education concerning this principle, there cannot be the results which so many of our great pioneers have worked for. And this principle is far different to what so many people seem to think.

Divine communion does not merely mean contact with those who inhabit the spirit world. Such contact can be, and indeed often is, anything but spiritual or divine. When dawns the day, and dawn it must, when Spiritualism enters into its own, then we may rest assured that spiritual communion will not then be used to camouflage fortune telling.

When the moment is ripe for soul to commune with soul, love — that wondrous yet terrible thing — enters into its own true day. This is the holy, sacred moment the soul had always known would come, the moment solemn and still yet so gloriously alive. It is the soul's pulse in rhythm and in harmony with the very soul of the universe. This moment has to be else is our love meaningless, empty and but a wicked mockery of every noble thought and lofty feeling of pure mind. Through the misty veils of death the undying voice of love calls aloud, "I still live." Thus love penetrates love and we behold an interpenetration of worlds. This is true communion.

Now there is seen and felt a new faith. For faith we must always have, if we are to evolve onward and upward. The world of today lives chiefly upon a useless, negative faith. Only when faith has its roots set in the knowledge of spiritual communion can it become the positive force it needs must be.

So is felt and known true and real humility, for now the mark of a pretentious humility, false and unnatural, must be cast away. How we have misused this word! In an attempt to lend virtue to our lazy, cowardly approach to life's problems, we claim humility to excuse our lack of talent, effort and ability. We are born with a power which defies limitation and we insult our God when we exclaim, "Who are we that we should dare invite men or powers so great into our presence?"

You may enter into the presence of the wisest and yet be able to instruct them. You have something to give and yet receive of all men in all time; only then may you claim interpenetrative philosophy is true. We should use our communion boldly.

Personal Responsibility.

Now it is that we discern in our philosophy, shape, form and pattern. All love penetrates its warming, nourishing way in our teachings and into our lives, as we become able to perceive with a thinking mind and a feeling heart, each richly serving the other. Then we begin to see how our philosophy can succeed where all others have failed. We now find ourselves able to perceive some of the tremendous implications of our next principle, Personal Responsibility.

It must surely now be obvious that our personal needs, wants and desires must actively concern themselves with all men all the time. With every word we speak, each thought we become conscious of, all action, all deeds, we express only part of the word, deed, and thought. We are making use of what has been made ready by other men of other years and climes. Well might we ask ourselves, "Do we make the best use of what was made ready for us?"

Shakespeare reached his heights because of men who, hundreds of years before he was born, made ready the path for him to tread. Men who evolved language, planned systems and methods of writing, men of history all shared in the responsibility and thus earned some place in the story.

Men of tomorrow will tread this way too. Much of what they will think and do will largely depend upon us. We are responsible for the future. With love alive in our beings, we can appreciate the need for the truly great soul, the need of the pure mind, the need of the upright, noble character, the need of understanding aright our next principle.

Compensation and Retribution.

Nature will not be cheated. Pay less than life demands and that much less will you receive of life. The ancient idea preached by orthodox religion of Heaven and Hell is an exaggerated fantasy of an eternal truth. The ancient doctrine of Nemesis is correct. The world is whole and life is one. What excess goes to the north, that much less remains in the south. Justice, that evasive will o' the wisp, is not after all a shadow, but a real law of the universe. The day may be long, the hour late, but justice walks behind you. Run your fastest, you will never be beyond her reach.

"What will you have of life?" quoth the gods. "Take it. Take it, and pay for it." Yes, what with envy you long would gaze upon is all yours. Take it, it is yours. Life does not beckon you forward and then say she is sold out. The storehouse of nature is ever open. Her only demand is that you pay the fair price.

This is a hard lesson for the instinctive, lust-filled passions of the human race to learn, but learn it we must. These instincts must be educated and directed into their higher channels. By a love, pure and unsullied, they must be coaxed and drawn into their higher realm wherein they may fulfil their high and noble destiny.

Deep indeed go the roots of this almighty, all powerful philosophy. Try as you will, you cannot escape from a single principle. In each one, all therein abide. In each one the others with

200

new force and freshness reappear, and each is only real and true because the others are.

So in the law of compensation and retribution we are taught again: not my way, not my will, but the Father's. Desire is awake and alive within you, but slowly by degrees, perhaps painfully, desire must be penetrated by a pure holy will. Desire of the physical must be blended into and become at one with desire of the mental. Desire of the mental must become at one with the spiritual desire. Spiritualism should be lived as a spiritual discipline.

A Pathway of Eternal Progress.

So there appears open before us an eternal pathway of progressive, evolving life. Having evolved thus far, man at last becomes man. Love, which for so long had been the submissive servant of instinctive passion-filled desire, speaks aloud in a voice unmistakable, clear and true: declaring itself the master, demanding obedience to its all-powerful will, content no longer with the artificial, slave no more to habit, custom or convention.

Thus the truly great soul is alive on our earth, walking a pathway of eternal goodness and love, content with nothing which will fail to prove itself true.

The eternal pathway is a pathway of eternal search. It is a pathway of eternal adventure. Nourished in this philosophy we can live our day fearless and unafraid. When the hard weather and storms and stresses of life hurl themselves against us, we shall be unhurt. Failure does not exist; there can never be defeat. What may seem so is only incidental. The eternal falling down and breaking apart is but an eternal building up and fitting together.

As Spiritualists, we must live through our difficulties as if they are glorious opportunities for progress.

How do we achieve a positive future for Spiritualism?

Firstly, we must realise that Spiritualism is about becoming. The time for a fuller Spiritualism will come when the time is right. It cannot be forced. However, it can be prepared for.

We must become more understanding of ourselves.

We must learn that a loving environment is essential for spiritual growth.

We must learn that each individual requires his own time and space to grow.

We must understand that it is only natural to carry with us remnants of older beliefs and fears when we first adopt Spiritualism as our own, and that these remnants will only be cast aside gradually.

Secondly, we must teach. We need to teach people to think, to question, to answer, to master facts. Only then will the thoroughly studied Seven Principles begin to yield their fuller significance.

We need to teach people to cast aside old ideas when new truth dawns.

We need to teach them to work hard for understanding, to accept only the highest standards.

We must teach Spiritualism as spiritual discipline in every aspect of life.

Why must we teach? Because we are all responsible for our futures. We must teach that too.

Thirdly, to our mediums we must say:

Put truth — not popularity — first.

Work at your calling with a holy dedication.

Widen out the whole concept of mediumship. The world is your seance room. All men are your sitters.

We must say, widen your concept of communion. It is communication with Spirit, but it is becoming one with Spirit too. It is touching God.

This preparation is the price we pay for Spiritualism coming into its own. This is the price we pay for man to grow into his new freedom.

Chapter Twenty Three

THE ETERNAL THEME

WHETHER you think of a theme in terms of music or poetry, or even restaurant design, it is an idea which runs constantly through different forms of expression, like an idea which you try to explain using many examples. In a symphony a theme may be a recurrent phrase or melody; in poetry it is a central idea expressed in varieties of figurative language; and in interior design it will be an idea expressed in a motif, pattern, shape, colour scheme or texture.

In each case, the theme recurs: it holds together the work of art as it is developed, and becomes the dominant idea within the piece. Once you are made aware of the theme, you will understand more fully the significance of the experience you are going through.

Life too has a theme which constantly recurs throughout the expression which we call creation. When we are aware of its theme, we may begin to understand the significance of the life we are living, and our life will become more full. We may even become more enthusiastic about it.

When music speaks to you, what does it say? When poetry moves you, what is its message? What truth does visual art declare before your very eyes? Before you answer, you must experience. Another's answer is not good enough. Only when you reach into life and experience it richly and wholeheartedly will you know its eternal theme. Until then, you may rest fairly content with just knowing about it.

There will come a time, if it has not yet arrived, when in amidst the unending flow you will find yourself pausing to question the deeper, fuller meaning of life. In such a moment you will wonder, and you struggle deeply to perceive this theme of life. You will want to distinguish amongst apparent chaos a pattern and direction.

There has to be pattern and order before we can understand anything at all. If one day, leaves grew on trees, and on another day on our shoes, and later still they sparkled in the sky, we could neither identify nor understand them. They only become significant to us because their pattern makes them predictable and lends them constancy.

Think of music. It is essentially sound, but even the simplest tune would be incomprehensible to us if all its notes sounded at once. It only becomes music when pattern and principle are imposed upon the sound. Insist that the notes come in sequence, with a certain progression; that each has its own rhythm and is accompanied by other harmonious notes. Then you have music.

Communication is not communication without the pattern and principles of language. It is not meaningful unless each collection of sounds is given an established meaning: there has to be a known vocabulary which is shared between the communicators. That same vocabulary has to be organised in such a way that sense can be drawn from it: thus grammar is required.

It is when the vibration of light energy is broken down into colour that we have the possibility of vision, but again, without the existence of pattern and principle, we should be at a loss to understand it. To make sense of vision, we need colour and shape, form and perspective. Only then can we make sense of what we see.

The very fact that we are aware of our surroundings and our lives and ourselves, demonstrates that there is pattern and principle in life too: an eternal theme if you like. So what then is this principle?

It is the principle of evolution. The principle behind all life is that it is growing all the time. In what way do I think it is growing? It is growing in consciousness. All energy and matter that exists in whatever form, is evolving in consciousness — becoming more aware if you like, more sensitive. All existence is not only becoming more aware of itself and other energies and other matter. All existence is evolving in consciousness towards

204

God.

Now to me, God is the sum of all knowing, all loving, all creating. To me the eternal theme of life is that life in every form is growing towards total consciousness — God consciousness. That is the theme of all life, and the pattern of all life can be traced in all the growth, development and change that is all around you.

The grain of sand, the corn of rice, the speck of dust or blade of grass, each earthly glow-worm or heavenly star, the moon above or the waters below: all things which exist are vital components of life's eternal pattern. Yet each pattern which man's struggling, groping mind perceives seems but some hint of a fuller pattern and that pattern seems far from his reach when he doesn't understand the eternal theme of life. Thus, in his moment of questioning, man often feels that his hand is reaching out for light in a world of perpetual dark.

In this mood, tense and still, there come feelings which no word, nor mind, nor heart can explain; moments when man acknowledges that the very fact which allows him to question or wonder is, of itself, a miracle. Great and majestic are these moments when life seems neither right nor wrong, but simply inevitable. In a manner breathless and with awe, man may stand confounded, and with Wordsworth he too shall say:

"Oft in my way I stood still, though but a casual

"Passenger, so much have I felt the awe-fulness of life."

This stillness, and the recognition, however vague, of the scale of life, are early steps in the individual's awareness of life's eternal theme. Be the mood or the moment what it may, certain laws at last become visible.

1. Life — moving, breathing, living life, constant in its flow, vigorous, animating life — exists.

2. Its mood and habit is growth.

3. Its growth is subject to law.

4. The pulse of living life is intention. Behind all life, behind growth and its laws, there is that which suggests a design. Somewhere beneath or above or within that which has been made visible, there abides a pattern. That pattern is intention.

5. Behind the intention there abides the designer, the Grand Architect: God.

So life exists. It is characterised by growth. The growth is subject to law. The law is willed by God. These basic principles suggest that a constructive system of philosophy can be evolved. They suggest that no matter how bewildering, confusing or perplexing our questions are, there are answers to them.

If a philosophy is worth possessing, it is also worth giving up something for. What do we need to give up in order to possess such a philosophy? We need to give up superstition, old patterns of thought which now prove to be false; we need to give up the idea that creation is the result of anything connected with chance or accident. If we cannot give up these notions, we must renounce our claim to a philosophy based upon the eternal theme of evolution of consciousness.

But if we are bold, we shall determine to understand that the governing laws and principles of life on its larger scale mimic or reflect the governing laws and principles on its smallest scale. We shall learn that what is true of the mass is true of each unit or cell. Each cell and each person, every moment and every day is subject to law. As Voltaire said, "Chance is a word void of sense, nothing can exist without cause."

As far as I can understand it, that ultimate cause is the will of God. Without that there is no law, no existence, no growth, no life. It is because all existence has one source that there can be an eternal theme throughout all life.

It is ironic though that thoughtful individuals seldom see the sameness or connectivity in life; they see in life its contradictions instead. When they see too many contradictions, they may find themselves overwhelmed into thinking that there is no certainty, order or eternal theme running through life.

It seems that down through the long corridors of time, philosophers have struggled successfully to explain away the inevitable paradoxes and apparent contradictions which every new system of thought introduces. They have no sooner declared that God can do all things than they discover that God cannot — for example — break His own laws.

As we watch philosophy at work then, we could say that all philosophy can be divided into two parts: the first part is devoted to the building up of a new idea, and the second works at pulling it down again. This is hardly a creative or progressive pastime. Perhaps it is a waste of time.

Well, philosophy would be a waste of time if it never got anywhere. The same could be said of any individual's life when it seems to be full of checks and balances, of contradictions. The fact is, though, that each does get somewhere: each is progressing.

Think of a man with a heavy load on his back, walking in the face of a strong wind. He plods on slowly, striding out first to the right, then to the left, his body swaying a little from side to side as he goes. This movement from side to side may seem contradictory, but it is not, for the figure is steadily progressing towards his goal directly in front of him.

So it is with contradictory ideas and conflicting experiences. We seem to sway from one to another, but in fact we grow in understanding and consciousness as we live through it all. If growth is the principle of life, time is the pattern of it. We experience one thing after another, and so we live in time because time is just a measure of these experiences.

Time has often been called the great healer. In one sense, it is. When we are hurt, disappointed or frightened by an event, we are like our packman who strode far to the left. Life seems seriously out of balance. However, as one experience follows on after another (as time passes) we find ourselves facing a further experience: a pace to the right, so to speak.

If we are wise enough to understand that life is about learning, we shall learn from its apparent contradictions and come to terms with what has happened to us. We are growing and developing. To continue our analogy, we move onward towards our goal. Through time we do this, and as a result, time heals. Through time, God's law inevitably works out.

Nothing is beyond time's reach. On its throne sit the laws of life, assured of eternal security. Time, like life, is inevitable; boundless in its scope, infinite and without measure. Its constant, incessant flow is the grand equaliser of all men and all things. In time there are no high nor low, no great nor small. Pure of bias, free of prejudice, cold yet unsullied, its unwavering gaze is cast on all alike.

In vain attempts to set up their own system of time values,

societies experience moments of pain and bitter distress. This is because they look for perfection in the moment, completion in the instant. The temporal moment seems to thrust its dagger into the sensitive bosom of pure life. It looks sinister and cruel in its work. For a while, the face of society may appear to be scarred, strained, disfigured and tarnished, but the eternal face of time shall remain free from blemish and shall forever be untouched. Such is the essential difference between the eternal and the temporal.

The philosophy of Spiritualism, embracing the principles I mentioned earlier, endeavours to face up to the difficulties of life's contradictions. It succeeds in tracing amongst the mass of these contradictions, some strands of the theme of life: the evolution of consciousness.

These strands of life's learning after being submitted to every conceivable form of test, remain unbroken. They show that the fundamental laws of life are, in the end, undisturbed and unmoved by all forms of accident or "chance" events.

Spiritual law proceeds in the face of all events to execute its will: relentlessly and with compelling force. The strength of these laws of life lies in the fact that no event whatsoever can thwart or cheat its unalterable purpose for through the process of time a counterbalance is always at hand to neutralise the effect of what seemed to be a chance event.

Physically and spiritually, you are free to choose what you will do. The result of your choice will be the inevitable result of law. You may choose to immerse your hand in water, but if you do, you cannot choose whether that hand will get wet: that it inevitable. However, you can learn from your experience if you want to, and that will help you to make a wiser choice in the future. Thus through the passage of time, your consciousness evolves.

An educationalist once told me that if you want to teach a pupil anything, you must first start from what the pupil knows — not what you want him to know. That may sound strange at first, so let's see what he meant.

Say you want to teach a child to calculate the area of a rectangle. You point to the long side and then to the shorter one. "You multiply that side by this side," you say. Now that is good teaching if your pupil already understands how to multiply, and has mastered his times tables. But if he is still learning to add, you have done nothing but confuse him. To be effective, you need to start at the same point as your pupil has reached. Only then can you lead him beyond that point into a further understanding.

Similarly, he may find it difficult to make sense of the concept of a rectangle. In that case, the good teacher will use an example his pupil will already be familiar with. The teacher might start off with a pack of butter, a matchbox, or a brick, and develop the concept of a rectangle from one of those.

Spiritualist philosophy works along the same lines. It starts from man and leads him out towards God, rather than starting with God and linking God back to man.

One of the most significant indications arising from the threads of our eternal theme of life that our philosophy is able to take hold of is the fact that all spiritual laws seem principally concerned with man. He and he alone is the key to the enigmas of the universe. All problems of life are reduced to the capacity of man to understand them, at least as far as man is concerned! And so it should be for he has to start with what he knows. The first thing he can truly hope to understand is himself.

Some things never change. The quest of the ancient sage is the quest of present day philosophy. For man to learn anything of the meaning of life, he must first learn of himself. And what is he?

He is an animal. He is known as human because of certain distinctive qualities. Being possessed of attributes unknown to bird or beast, he is considered to have evolved above their level. Nevertheless, in the first instance, man is an animal.

Man is a hungry animal. He is equipped with desires and possessiveness. His first desire is for food. Without such a desire, he could not survive. His survival is ensured by a possessive nature which seeks to retain that which it has. "That's mine!" growls the dog to anyone who would dare approach his bone. "Mine!" cries the baby clutching tightly his toy. "Mine!" is the echo and re-echo constantly to be heard from each succeeding stage of man's growth and development. "Mine!" mutters the aspiring, ambitious emperor, his cold calculating eyes gazing out on to the country and the people below him.

Fundamentally, the characteristics of man the animal are

both sound and necessary. Without hunger, without his possessiveness, he would be lacking the instincts so essential for his
survival. He would lack will and desire so necessary to growth and
evolution. He would be without the ability to offer challenge to the
adverse conditions of life. Without the desire to possess and
acquire, the hope and dream of evolution would remain in embryo
state: silent, still and forever unfulfilled.

Man's animal nature can only be condemned when it is
expressed in excess or extremes. But his nature only begins to
serve its true purpose when it is realised that although man is an
animal, he is animal plus.

When his natural power is directed and channelled, man
becomes productive. In this sense, man the animal is a machine.
Fed with certain food, provided with chosen environments, cor-
responding emotions and impulses will invariably be fired and
stimulated into action. Circumstances and conditions of a set order
never fail to cause the individual or the mass to follow a given line
of action. There is a formula which will call man to worship. There
is a formula which always drives man to war.

If you throw the right switch, the mechanism moves into
action to supply the predicted product. It is perhaps not difficult to
understand that man is a machine in the physical sense, but not so
easy and certainly less pleasant to look upon our own emotional or
sexual or nervous or even mental selves as mechanical in their
constitution. It is even less easy on our understanding and our pride
to admit that our anger and our tolerance, the sweetness of our
virtue or the sour taste of our vices, our every mood and reaction
are but mechanical in their natures.

At this thought, we rush on to say that man is machine plus.
He has an intellect. Yet even the realms of the intellect find man
bound to the mechanical order of his being. In strict accordance to
his type (astrological or otherwise) each man follows a set line of
intellectual tastes and appetites.

Tied to the traits of his type, certain events invariably bore
and tire him, whilst other events never fail to thrill and excite.
Within the firm grip of his type there are conclusions to which
every Tom will readily admit, and every Harry deny, whilst always
is Dick without interest. Each Tom, each Harry and each Dick are

in their set grooves and with mechanical regularity give their ready-made "Yes" or "No."

The giving of opinions is often mistaken for the arriving at them. When I tell you what I think, you may well assume that my intellect has been at work. It may have been, but only superficially. The intellect need not be in full operation at all. You can only begin to guess how hard it has been working when I begin to tell you why I think as I do, or how I arrived at my conclusions. And I can only be sure that my intellect is alive and well when it brings about changes in my life, my approach, my feelings and so on.

Voicing opinions is only the first flickerings of intellect. It too will grow and develop with use. The intellect of itself is cold, unfeeling and without heart. It is without bias and free from taint of prejudice. Its sole task is to search, to probe, to unravel and analyse. The man who can truly claim to be an intellectual may not know a great deal, but he will constantly question, and never be afraid to accept the consequences of his answers once he has found them.

The potential value of the intellect is tremendous; ways hitherto untrod are made open to every man; new and loftier heights are scaled. To intellect's penetrating, persistent, searching gaze the secrets of the universe are one by one revealed.

Once channelled, the power of the animal allows the productive machine of man to be driven. As the products of the machine are selected, man the intellectual can begin to function. Now we can begin to trace the development of the eternal theme in life as conscious grows.

Our picture of man is not yet complete, however. Down through the long passage of years, the war cry of all great reforms has been,"Liberty! Freedom! Let us set free enslaved man!" Revolutions have arisen and still arise to free men from the vice-like grips of oppressive dictators and regimes. One by one the bonds have been cut, the chains removed, the shackles unlocked; but the newly acquired liberty, the new born freedom, finds man more of a slave than before.

We begin to wonder just how possible meaningful evolution really is because in the free world man has offered himself to ever newer lords and mistresses, offering them blind, unquestioning obedience. When freed from one tyranny, man soon finds another. He becomes a slave to habit, fashion or convention; slave to the systems which granted his freedom; slave to the methods of rush and scramble — the ever quickening tempo of life.

Men's new master is fear. His new mistress is indifference and selfishness. Fear of other people, fear of their thoughts, their comments and opinions; indifferent to the vastness of wondrous possibilities which lie open before him, indifferent to the lot of others; and selfish with gifts intended to be shared. When can he evolve then? When he dares to be free.

When man permits himself flight from the prison house of his own making, the magic power of imagination stakes its claim to occupy the throne of man's mind in consort with the intellect. For man is also a dreamer. Under the touch of this strange, enchanting wand, all men become poets and in turn become lord, master and king when they so choose.

Imagination, like life, like time and all other basic patterns traced by the eternal theme, is inevitable. Of itself alone, it is unable to be of lasting benefit to man; to achieve success, it is dependent upon harmonious relationships with all other parts of this amazingly complex being called man. Animal, mechanical, intellectual and imaginative: all elements have to work together.

And men too must work together for evolution to be significant. Man is not merely a human being, he is part of humanity. "I am a man," said Terrance, "and whatever concerns humanity is of interest to me."

All men, whatever their class or their type are worthy of being understood, however difficult that might be. Snobbery is another name for stupidity or blindness. Dickens was very near the mark when he wrote, "It will be generally found that those who sneer habitually at human nature and effect to despise it, are among its worst and least pleasant samples."

In order to evolve, to grow, to touch the greater heights, to gain the larger freedom, to become the master instead of the slave of pain and disease, man must serve not himself but humanity. This is because humanity is larger than the individual.

If a man were only to serve his own needs, his consciousness and his thought would never range beyond the single, the individual.

Man can hardly expect to evolve consciousness of God if he concentrates wholly upon himself. He has to extend his capacity beyond his own singleness, beyond his own personal limitations, beyond all these to other human beings and then to humanity itself. His own self will always be an endless source of information and inspiration for him, but for variety and contrast, he has to look to humanity and become involved in it — and serve it.

Aristotle was one day reproached for giving help to an unworthy person. He gave the perfect reply, "I did not give to the man, but to humanity."

The eternal theme of evolution unfolds further yet. As man becomes involved with humanity, slowly there stirs within him a sensation which in due time evolves into a feeling of respect, regard and affection for other men and other things. Stirred from its deep and heavy slumber, conscience begins to unfold and become awake.

In becoming aware of his relation to humanity, man makes his first attempt to become a moralist. This is the moment which with great patience, the untiring cause of life has toiled and waited for, the moment when man at last questions, "Is my action good?"

The victory of this newly awakened conscience of his is neither swift nor sure. Man the moralist does not find himself faced with only one straightforward question: he finds himself submerged in a boundless ocean of perplexing enigmas. He stands confronting not just one enemy, but a whole multitude of foes (if difficult situations can be thought of as foes). All his instincts, tastes and appetites, every impulse, lust and passion of his are there to do battle with his conscience.

The voice of conscience calls out for an answer to its dilemma and experiments in varied ways to overcome these formidable foes. It experiments with suppression of desire, but this is not the answer. Suppressed desire with its force and energy increased by repression, will only knock on other doors.

Schooled and calculated indifference is not the answer either. This method only disturbs and upsets the whole emotional structure of man. Nor is the intellectual approach for the intellect is possessed of one considerable failing. Napoleon is an outstanding example of this. If only his heart had borne any proportion to his brain, he would have been one of the greatest men in all history. Intellect without feeling and caring cannot be the proper measure of what is right and wrong.

The struggle of conscience is a demanding one, yet though hard and difficult the way, even in the darkest of ages there has always been a sufficiency of moral victory to ensure that evolution proceeds. There are always those who emerge above the mass and by the sheer virtue of their beings, demonstrate the existence of the Eternal Theme.

Complete and absolute moral victory seems ever evasive. Even the saints have to content themselves with faint tastes of this unreachable prize. But we all may continue to strive and thus to grow.

We began with the animal nature. It grew through the stages of productiveness, intellect, imagination and conscience. We have followed its path. Now we shall ask how it grows.

The fulfilment of life's eternal theme demands obedience to certain positive commandments or rules. The first rule is "I must be fed."

The life in man must be fed wisely and with care, because it derives its energy, force and power from the food with which it is provided.

There are three basic ways in which man must be fed: Food and water, air and mental impressions.

He requires ordinary food and drink, for without it, man would not survive. Without food he could last only six weeks or so; without water, no more than a few days. Without air he could not live more than a few minutes.

But what about mental impressions? Without impressions of any kind, man would instantly cease to be alive for at all times there must be parts of man's organism which are possessed of awareness. His impressions must not only be constant: they have to be varied if his sanity is to remain in tact.

Feeding by food, air and impressions stimulates and encourages the activity of the life forces within man. Force and energy is generated, the many emotional centres are called into awareness. By food, air and impressions, they have breathed into them the breath of life; and by imagination they are given increase.

214

For you see, the satisfying of one set of desires enables another set to grow and then to demand fulfilment.

To have breathed into you the breath of life is to be filled with the urge and desire to live. Feeding forms pockets of energy within man, and from these deposits of force all the instincts, feelings, passions are given life. With ever increasing demand in their voices, they cry out and plead of man's essence to be used. These centres of man's being are aware of one all-powerful urge, one overwhelming desire: the urge and desire for action. Here are sources of energy that have been made alive and they intend to live.

They have no conscience, no ethics, no moral code. Here, surely, the appalling danger of the weak, ineffective, uneducated ego is made apparent. Man the animal, the machine, the slave, the hungry, the ambitious, the desiring, wanting man is at large in the world.

Knowledge is the answer to this grim danger. The master self or the ego of man can only fulfil its true function and become an effective force when the second positive commandment of human growth is obeyed: I must have knowledge.

A sufficiency of knowledge will, in due time, shock the ego into an awareness of its true position. Meanwhile, the soul of the universe is calm and unafraid, for there abides within man, awaiting the soil of knowledge and culture to be sufficiently fertilised, a centre of energy, force and power more wonderful than anything else in life.

"I must have love: must love and be loved" is the next commandment for spiritual growth.

It is a quality of eternal being. Love is the crowning glory of universal law and is the grand apex of all life. Love is the texture of the soul and the fabric of love is eternity. It is timeless and without age. By love is man's ego made truly, gloriously alive; through love he catches glimpses of the eternal reality.

The ineffable cause of life has been conveyed by every great philosopher in the form of some tangible symbol that man could understand. It was represented by Thales as water, by Anaximander as air, as thought by Anaxagoras, as fire by Zoroaster, and by later philosophers as love.

All were right, but only partly so. For this cause which gave

215

to all men the flavour of divinity, refuses to be restricted to a name. This bloodstream of all life, this parent of universal love, permits man to be lifted up high on his rightful throne from whence he stands, gazing with trembling, excited amazement upon visions of permanency in life. When he loves as his creator loves, man is no longer merely an animal, machine, slave, mind, imagination and conscience: he is a living soul. A living, growing soul.

The process continues. Love is also hungry and must always be fed by knowledge. Ideas, faith and belief will not suffice for long. Beyond these infant stages, there is knowledge intense and real. It is intense and real because it is experienced directly. Love must have such knowledge or it will fall victim of spiritual amnesia. Weak, limp and helpless, love starved of knowledge will become lifeless and ineffective in man. Love is fed by wisdom, and wisdom by love.

There is only one possible way for such knowledge to come to man. Only one way which permits the soul of man to be brought face to face with naked, unvarnished truth. One way for man to know with all the intensity and drama of certainty, that his vision of continuity in life was not just faith, or a hope, or a dream.

The way is mediumship: this is the only answer which can bring a sense of equilibrium to the world philosophies and religions. The reality of mediumship can no longer be held in dispute. Astute minds of every clime and age have declared the truth; science ceases to be science when it denies this remarkable fact.

The soul of man can attune itself to the souls of other men, can enjoy moments of affinity with souls of other lands and ages, with souls evolved above this mortal, earthly hour. Mediumship, when pure and not sullied with a morbid curiosity, enables man to behold the purpose in life, brings to him the knowledge that love — and therefore life — have their roots in a permanent reality. This reality is the continuous evolution of the spirit of man towards God. It is the reality of no death. It is the reality of a spiritual identity, not a physical one.

And yes, of course, when we learn of our true identity, how much more is made clear to us. Bodies, times and places are no more than patterns woven by the eternal theme. We use them to express the soul which is us. When they fade and pass, it is to no

216

avail, for we are constant still.

Every time you love another person, an animal, the environment: that is mediumship. When you care, when you pray for help or ask space for an answer, when you need to heal: that is mediumship. You use every aspect of yourself as a channel for your love, your wisdom, your spirit so that you can touch — spiritually touch — that other being. How else can we truly know another person when all the physical things about them are constantly changing? We are mediums all, and through our mediumship we learn and we love and then we grow.

It is when we need feed spiritually and there is no-one around us who can help, that we find ourselves reaching out to souls no longer in a physical body. That is when the more obvious forms of mediumship occur. That is when we are reminded most meaningfully that our spirits evolve beyond the death of the physical body. Mediumship is simply the process of spiritual communication.

Mediumship is not a recent acquirement. Without mediumship, religion would not have been born, no philosophy would have evolved, no science be known to man. All men are mediums. Through this facility the poetry of the world is written, and its art expressed. Yet all the while the world awaits the fulfilment of this mediumship's highest function: communion with God.

This fulfilment has been suppressed by vested interests, held back by militant, power-seeking rulers who took control of the established religions throughout history.

The scientific, philosophical and religious implications of true mediumship have been withheld or camouflaged beyond recognition by war-minded leaders and position-seeking politicians. The truth as revealed through mediumship was not wanted by those whose hands reached out to clutch and grasp the glory of a temporal and fleeting moment.

The people were thus fed with superstition, doped with ceremonial, pomp and ritual, and made content to bask in the false light of a teaching systematically evolved to ensure that they were kept in ignorance of their true heritage.

Growth and evolution, however, are facts, and be the moment soon or be it late, the knowledge of man's birthright shall find its

217

way into his higher consciousness. Recognition of his mediumship is a highly significant point in his evolution.

It is at this point, with vision enlarged and emotions aglow that the soul of man is ready to inhale the breath, life and wisdom of other and higher spheres. It is at this point he is ready to meet in ethereal embrace souls who have journeyed on beyond the limitations of earth life. Ready to break free from the fetters which bound him and held him slave; ready to dispense with the dope of superstition, to see beyond the thin and useless veil of pompous ceremony and artificial pretence.

Then he will be ready to experience at first hand the eternal theme of life, and feel its radiance bless him and make hallowed his intimacy with other worlds. For he lives and grows always.

Whither goest thou, oh soul? I go from whence I came: to God which is my home. I return through the many spheres, realms, kingdoms and worlds to God — the womb of all life and wherein my roots are set.

Each step of the way shall be life, and every breath which I breathe shall be love. I am going neither where time nor space confines or restricts, where all worlds are but one world and all men are brothers. I journey along with the eternal theme, to continue with vigour and robust health this great adventure called life.

Chapter Twenty Four

HARVEST

NOW, if you were to ask me what was the most important thing I have ever done or experienced, I doubt if I could answer you. Who is to say what is important? You can never tell. For something may have an effect that you may never be aware of. You have to live life as if all things are important — the great and the small — because in the way of things, they are all important.

But the most significant time of the church year for me is the time of harvest. It appeals so much because it so reflects the natural philosophy that is Spiritualism.

It is a time for gathering in the fruits of experience, and enjoying those fruits, sharing them with others. It is a time for understanding that change is an inevitable part of the natural cycle of life. It is a time to relish that change. And perhaps above all, it is the time a Spiritualist can embrace the notion of death wholeheartedly, because he sees it for exactly what it is — the very earliest beginnings of the next cycle, the glorious birth of our new potential.

Share with me now, the words one student shared with me:
The sighing scythe hushes the last whisper
Of the falling ears of corn
They are gold come from clay
An alchemist's prayer, answered.
Ask now for your daily, precious bread
And it shall be given —
Not freely, but
After grinding pain refines
And weltering heat makes the dead rise again.

Break bread with me now —
In Communion —
That I might rejoice
At the golden life resurrected
In your eyes
And your smile
And in the Life the Reaper will cut down
But never end.